OAK ISLAND
and its lost treasure

THIRD EDITION

GRAHAM HARRIS AND LES MacPHIE

Formac Publishing Company Limited
Halifax

Formac Publishing Company Limited recognizes the support of the Province of Nova Scotia through the Department of Communities, Culture and Heritage. We are pleased to work in partnership with the Culture Division to develop and promote our culture resources for all Nova Scotians. We acknowledge the support of the Canada Council for the Arts which last year invested $24.3 million in writing and publishing throughout Canada. We acknowledge the financial support of the Government of Canada through the Canada Book Fund for our publishing activities.

Photo Credits: *Ancient Carpenters' Tools*: p.90, p.91; Canadian Department of Energy, Mines and Resources: p.100; Dodge Photo: p.67 (bottom); Estate of Thomas Gardiner: p.167; *Halifax Herald-Chronicle*: p.104; Les MacPhie: p.137 (top, middle and bottom), p.138; National Portrait Gallery: p.174; *The Halifax Herald*: p.67 (top); Triton Alliance: p.74, p.88 (top and bottom), p.89 (top and bottom), p.90, p.106, p.113, p.113, p.115, p.117, p.118 (top and bottom), p.119 (top and bottom), p.125 (left and right), p.129; Dennis Gummer: p. 173; National Gallery: p. 187.

Library and Archives Canada Cataloguing in Publication
Harris, Graham, 1937–
Oak Island and its lost treasure / Graham Harris and Les MacPhie. — 3rd ed.

Includes bibliographical references and index.
Issued also in an electronic format.
ISBN 978-1-4595-0259-8

1. Oak Island Treasure Site (N.S.)—History. 2. Treasure troves—Nova Scotia—Oak Island (Lunenburg)—History. I. MacPhie, Les, 1941– II. Title.

FC2345.O23H37 2013 622'.190971623 C2013-901343-1

Formac Publishing Company Limited
5502 Atlantic Street
Halifax, Nova Scotia B3H 1G4
www.formac.ca

Printed and bound in Canada

Table of Contents

Acknowledgements

Many individuals have contributed to the preparation of this book by aiding us in the collection of research data and pursuing obscure lines of enquiry at our request. Several libraries and public institutions have also given unstinting assistance. Without such support this book would be less comprehensive and the poorer for it. Of special satisfaction has been the cooperation of Oak Island enthusiasts with whom we have communicated.

In this third edition we would especially like to acknowledge the massive contribution made by Peter Kirkham of London, through his invaluable research into British military archives; Bill Glen of Bonshaw, Prince Edward Island, through his work on immigrant ships of the eighteenth century; and the assistance provided by the Royal Engineers Library, Chatham, Kent.

We would also like to acknowledge the interest, encouragement and support provided by the management of SNC-Lavalin Inc., Montreal, and the staff who assisted in the preparation of the illustrations. Particular thanks are due to Mihai Staicu for his excellent work on drafting the figures.

We are thankful also for the support and cooperation of Colleen Wormald and the editorial staff of Formac Publishing for their contribution to this third edition.

List of Figures

Preface

Almost two decades have elapsed since we commenced our studies into what is commonly known as 'the mystery of Oak Island.' We have sifted through countless documents, and have followed many avenues of enquiry directed towards solving this age-old 'mystery.' It was Roger Ascham (1515–68), a learned Elizabethan, who remarked, "By experience, we find a short way by a long wandering." In our attempts to resolve 'who' did 'what,' 'why' and 'when' on Oak Island our wanderings have proved long indeed. However, our work has reached the point where new findings justify the printing of this latest enlarged edition of *Oak Island and its Lost Treasure.*

The first edition of this book indicated an underground failure had befallen the original diggers of the Money Pit, with the implication that any treasure consigned to the security of its depths had proved impossible to recover. This led to the conclusion that the two main elements of the underground workings, namely the Money Pit shaft and the Flood Tunnel, were excavated by different parties decades apart.

The second edition presented new information relating to the identification of tools discovered in the Money Pit, to circumstances leading to the construction of the Flood Tunnel, to the period during which it was excavated and identification of the military engineers involved.

This third edition includes an entirely new chapter on the role of the British military on Oak Island. Over a two-year period a scheme was implemented with the intent of ensuring the treasure, lost sixty years earlier, would be flooded for posterity and rendered impossible to recover. The cloak of secrecy surrounding the project, its duration and cost, is a measure of the vast wealth that had been lost. The final chapter contains an assessment of the value of the lost treasure still awaiting recovery. This edition includes four new figures related to the role of the British military, and many of the second edition figures have been updated.

There are many difficulties confronting the researcher of the written record as it relates to Oak Island. Many source documents, particularly newspapers, contain inconsistencies of fact, and we have used judgment in their interpretation in determining the sequence of events. On occasions there are discrepancies in identifying the proper locations of some of the early exploration shafts and the order in which they were dug. The shaft identification system adopted here therefore follows that of R.V. Harris in the second edition of his book, *The Oak Island Mystery*. A complete list of the shafts put down by treasure-seekers since 1795, when first signs of old underground workings were detected, is given in the appendix in chronological order, together with a summary of the major drilling campaigns and excavations.

The first part of this book focuses upon the various treasure-seeking ventures on the island following the discovery of 1795, when signs of underground workings were detected on the island. This is a fascinating history in itself. The second part deals with the circumstances that appear to have led to the selection of Oak Island as a repository for the treasure, which is of equal fascination as it relates to political intrigue for the purpose of revolution.

Will the lost treasure of Oak Island ever be recovered? That is a question which only time can tell. The forces of nature, which led to the loss of the treasure in the first place, will have to be overcome by careful engineering if disaster is to be avoided a second time.

Sherlock Holmes, the fictional detective, once said, "If the facts don't agree with the theory, alter the theory." We believe the thesis expounded in this book regarding the origin of the treasure, the circumstances of its loss, and the efforts to cover up its very existence, accounts for all the known facts both technical and historical. We readily admit our inability to present the incontestable proof which would resolve the Oak Island mystery once and for all. Our hope is that one day it will be found; in the meantime our dilemma is akin to that of Shakespeare's Othello:

So prove it,
That the probation bear no hinge, nor loop,
To hang a doubt on.

Dates given in this book have been converted, where necessary, to conform to the present dating system, i.e. the Gregorian Calendar, first adopted by Catholic countries in 1582. The British continued to use the older Julian Calendar up to 1752.

Graham Harris, Bedeque, Prince Edward Island, Canada
Les MacPhie, Montreal, Quebec, Canada

Introduction

Each year thousands of tourists travel the scenic Lighthouse Route that skirts the rockbound South Shore of Nova Scotia. Their drive takes them through picturesque towns and villages nestled amidst numerous rivers, creeks and inlets that indent the rugged coast. The communities along this route bear testimony to the early days of settlement, when one of the first priorities was to seek safe and secure anchorage from the all-too-frequent storms that lash the region. One of the earliest communities was the Town of Chester (see Figures 1 and 2), which occupies a promontory jutting into Mahone Bay. It was first settled in the mid-eighteenth century.

One of the first things the curious visitor to Chester may hear about is the mystery of Oak Island. Lying directly against the western shore of Mahone Bay, this island presents a forbidding aspect with its profuse growth of somber conifers looming out of the often turbulent waters. In the past, the island supported a dense growth of red oaks, but few remain. Legend tells that Oak Island was the only island in the bay to support such a growth.

The British colonial administration gave a grant of land in 1759 to migrants from the Massachusetts Bay Colony who undertook to settle the Chester area, thereby becoming the first English-speaking residents of the region, after Halifax, to commence settlement in earnest. The grant was known as the Shoreham Grant, and covered an area of about 11½ miles by 15½ miles (see Figure 2). It is a huge area by today's standards, encompassing a vast tract of wilderness and many of the islands within the bay, including Oak Island. It was a mere thirty-six years after the signing of the land grant that unmistakable evidence was discovered that others had visited Oak Island in the past and used it for purposes other than settlement. To this date no one has determined these purposes, though theories abound.

Many books have been written about the mystery of Oak Island, and the average person may be excused for being somewhat confused by the numerous theories that are advanced. For 220 years the island has been the site of fruitless endeavours to unravel the mystery of 'who' buried 'what,' 'why' and 'when,' as buried within the depths of the island there is indeed something. The evidence is tantalising. Pirate treasure is favoured by many, though if truth be told there is little evidence that pirates ever buried much of their ill-gotten gains. Other theories have suggested vast caches of ancient treasure once belonging to the Egyptians, the Incas, the Mayans or the Aztecs, a sacred treasure with a Masonic or Templar connection, the crown jewels of Scotland

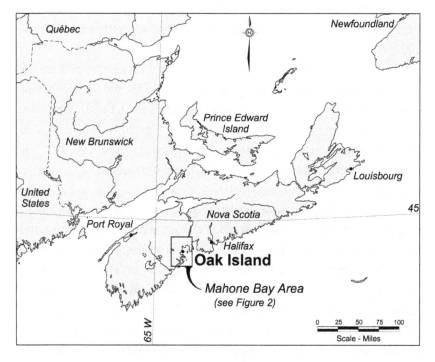

Figure 1
Map of Nova Scotia

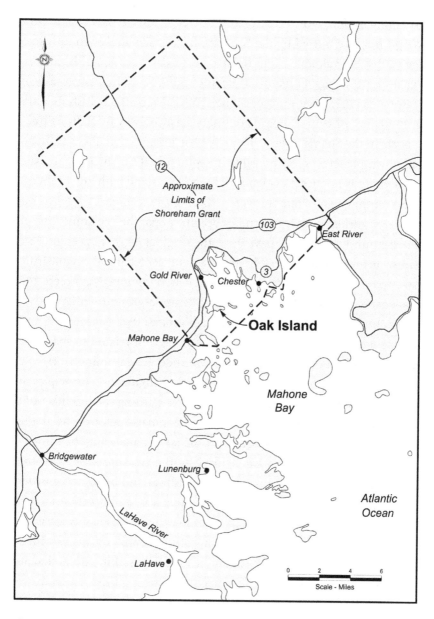

Figure 2

Map of Mahone Bay

and France, New World treasure plundered by Sir Francis Drake, New World treasure buried by the Spanish in extensive underground storage vaults, the valuable cargo from a storm-damaged Spanish galleon, Shakespeare's original manuscripts, the spoils from the British sack of Havana in 1762, large sums of money concealed by the British military in 1780 and, of course, hoards of booty stashed away by stalwart buccaneers of the Spanish Main. There is even a theory that aliens from an unknown planet were responsible. Despite this abundance of fantastic ideas, there is no direct evidence linking Oak Island with any of them.

Some time ago, while we were debating the technical evidence for the deep workings at Oak Island, it became apparent that some type of underground failure may have beset the original diggers. As engineers, whose professional careers in the field of geotechnical engineering have spanned the past fifty years, we felt well equipped to accept the challenge of investigating the mysterious underground works at Oak Island. Our collective experience includes major civil engineering and mining ventures on all five continents, much of it related to shaft and tunnel construction and the stability of underground mine workings. It seemed timely, therefore, to apply practical engineering principles in a serious attempt to sift myth from reality regarding the legends built up about the deep shaft at Oak Island, popularly referred to as the Money Pit. Accordingly, we set about the task of analysing the numerous records and accounts left behind by the treasure-seekers of the past, in an attempt to rationalize their findings and bring some order to the apparent present confusion. Our hope was, and continues to be, that our contributions might help to resolve this all-absorbing mystery.

We travelled a well-worn path, a path followed by many others who have written about Oak Island; but we followed it with a view to finding those technical clues that may have been missed. In truth we discovered little of the mystery with which the island had been credited. The investigation supported our first major premise that the Oak Island enterprise, for whatever reason it was first undertaken, had been subject to a serious failure related to the unique geological features of the island.

Having evaluated the technical reasons for the failure of the Money Pit, and assessed the likely period of its first excavation from the clues available, we scanned our history books searching for events that might have led to the selection of Oak Island for some secret enterprise. We were particularly attracted to a treasure-seeking expedition off the coast of Hispaniola led by Sir William Phips of Boston. Phips had been knighted by King James II of England in 1687 for his success in locating the wreck of one of Spain's most richly laden galleons, which had foundered during its homeward bound voyage in 1641. Phips brought back to the king a wealth in silver, but it was only a fraction of the wealth remaining in the stricken vessel. A return expedition to the wreck site in 1687–88 to retrieve more booty from the ocean's depths was reportedly fruitless. However, the circumstances surrounding this second visit are highly suspicious — so suspicious that there is more than a hint of conspiracy among the participants. Revolution was brewing in England against the autocratic rule of King James, and many viewed William, Prince of Orange, as a potential saviour. The year 1688 was the year of the Glorious Revolution when William invaded England and James fled his throne.

We made the link (based on circumstantial evidence) that the senior members of the return expedition of 1688 were part of a conspiracy, urged on by a certain Lord Charles Mordaunt, the 3rd Earl of Peterborough (one of the most colourful characters of the period), to ensure that part of the rich booty won from the wreck was to be held for William, Prince of Orange. It is postulated that the treasure was cached in the Money Pit at Oak Island with the intention of recovering it after the revolution proved successful.

A narrative account of the treasure-seeking exploits of Sir William Phips, and the conspiracy into which he was drawn, is given in *The Golden Reef of Sir William Phips* (Booksurge Publishing, 2005).

This historical context and the technical evidence from our findings supported our second major premise that the Money Pit workings had been excavated in two phases, with the possibility that several decades had elapsed between the two phases of work. The first phase was, of course, the Money Pit shaft, at the bottom of which would have been the treasure chambers. Following the loss of the treasure through geological reasons, and the presumed inability to recover that treasure after the revolution, the second phase ensured that no one else would ever recover the treasure, by linking the Money Pit shaft with the sea via a flood tunnel.

We can now say, based on considerable historical and circumstantial evidence, that the Money Pit phase of the underground workings, namely the vertical shaft extending into the underlying bedrock, was constructed by William Phips and the crew of his ship, the *Good Luck*, between August 1688 and the following January. After the subsequent loss of the treasure, which must have occurred in 1689 on the first recovery attempt after the revolution, further attempts would have been made over the succeeding years or decades. It is believed that the first major efforts to recover the lost treasure would have been made between 1689 and 1697. This is the period when Acadia was occupied by the British, after which it was returned to France. During this time King William created a corps of engineers whose clandestine activities remain unknown to this day, but which is believed to have been formed with the purpose of recovering the lost treasure. Their efforts failed for the geological forces at play were barely understood. The treasure was most assuredly lost.

Whether any further attempts were made at treasure recovery following 1697 is unknown, but in 1752 the British government dispatched a team of Cornish miners to Annapolis Royal, the old seat of government in Nova Scotia. This date preceded the proposed settlement of Lunenburg by one year. And Lunenburg is only ten miles from Oak Island as the crow flies!

The team of miners was led by one of the most celebrated British military tunnelling engineers of the period. The terms of his orders suggest the secret project upon which they were engaged to have been highly classified. This engineer and his team disappear from the record for two years after their arrival. The conclusion is drawn that the project concerned was construction of the renowned Flood Tunnel, the presence of which so greatly bedevilled early exploration activities. The date of construction for the Flood Tunnel can thus be judged as having taken place between the fall of 1752 and the summer of 1754, a period of eighteen months to two years. Following completion of the engineers' clandestine work, Oak Island was to remain virtually unexplored for the next forty-one years.

We will not know if our hypothesis is correct until the mystery of Oak Island is finally resolved by recovering that which is buried there. But if we are correct, there lies beneath the island a fantastic store of wealth, which, at the time of its burial, would have an estimated value equivalent to the annual budget of any European state of the seventeenth century. In today's terms the lost treasure is estimated to be about sixty million dollars.

The detailed results of our research are written, we trust, in language that any earnest reader may understand, however, for guidance, we include a glossary to help overcome any difficulties with unavoidable technical terms. The historical reasoning that led to the digging of the Money Pit in the first place and later construction of the Flood Tunnel is believed to be credible, even though the evidence is circumstantial. After all, conspirators are not renowned for ensuring a well-documented paper trail to disclose their nefarious activities!

CHAPTER 1
Dreams of Buried Treasure

Dream after dream ensues,
And still they dream that they shall still succeed
And still are disappointed
"Dreams, Empty Dreams" (Cowper)

It was a summer's day in June 1795 when young Daniel McGinnis went exploring on Oak Island and first discovered evidence of the Money Pit. For thirty-five years King George III had been on the throne of Great Britain and her territories, during which time great events had stirred the world. The American Revolution had lost Great Britain her New England colonies, and the French Revolution had shocked the civilized world with its indiscriminate and bloody slaughter. But all that lay in the past when Daniel McGinnis went exploring.

It is unlikely that the young McGinnis knew anything about the Shoreham Grant, which thirty-six years earlier included Oak Island as part of a large land transfer. Shoreham was the first name selected for what is now the Town of Chester. The Shoreham Grant was signed on October 18, 1759 by Charles Lawrence Esquire, Captain-General and Governor-in-Chief of Nova Scotia. The grant was made to a number of individuals, most of whom originated from the Massachusetts Bay Colony. The original copy of the grant consists of seven handwritten pages and includes the following curious phrase:

> Do by these Presents give grant and Confirm unto the
> several Persons hereafter named Seventy Shares & a half of
> Two hundred Shares or Rights whereof the said Township
> is to consist with all and all manner of Mines unopened

excepting Mines of Gold and Silver, precious Stones and
Lapis Lazuli in & upon the said Shares or Rights.

The credulous might be excused for believing the reference to gold
and silver applies to ores in their natural state. This interpretation
might even be extended to precious stones, though Nova Scotia was
not renowned at the time for the production of jewel stones, and is
never likely to be. However, only the gullible would believe this interpretation as relating to lapis lazuli, which is a highly treasured precious stone originating mainly from China and Central Asia, though
insignificant amounts can be found elsewhere. Lapis lazuli is bright
blue and softer than most precious stones and has been called the
'sapphire of the ancients.'

The usual way to exclude potentially valuable, but undiscovered
minerals from a land grant was to include the phrase "excepting
mines of gold, silver, lead, copper and coals." The exceptions included in the Shoreham Grant strongly suggest that reference was being
made to something other than valuable minerals in their native
or natural states. The inference is obvious: the exceptions refer to
treasure. Equally obvious is the conclusion that the government
was unable to recover that treasure for its own benefit, for whatever
reason.

The earliest land grant in which the curious phraseology appeared
regarding "Mines of Gold and Silver, precious Stones and Lapis
Lazuli," has been traced to one dated June 10, 1754, a year after the
settlement of Lunenburg. Thereafter the phrase became a standard
insertion into all such grants. Colonel Lawrence, who was responsible
for the settlement, and was later appointed to the post of Governor of
Nova Scotia, wrote in October 1754 that the settlers were beginning to
agitate for the right to mine gold and silver in the area:

The mines of gold, silver and precious stones were (entirely)
reserved to ye Crown, it being apprehended that ye search

after them could not probably be ye business of ye settlers
nor of ye prospect of them any encouragement to ye provisions [of] such settlement.

If our assertion is correct, that the Flood Tunnel was constructed
between the fall of 1752 and the summer of 1754, it would have been
contemporary with the establishment of Lunenburg. It is therefore not
surprising that rumour, loose talk and idle speculation would have
been the natural consequence. During this early period redcoats, i.e.
British military, were reported to be present on the island.

The earliest known written accounts of Daniel McGinnis's discovery
of 1795 appeared in local newspapers in the mid-nineteenth century,
some sixty-five to seventy years later. These accounts, probably based
on stories passed on for more than two generations, contain some
inconsistencies and, most likely, some embellishments. Various articles
published from 1861 to 1864 described the initial discovery and subsequent early diggings. Despite the contradictions in the accounts,
there is clear evidence that McGinnis stumbled upon a location where
previous visitors to Oak Island had carried out extensive underground
workings. His first thought may well have been of pirate treasure, as
accounts of Captain Kidd and his predations were legion at the time.

We are told that McGinnis penetrated the growth of massive oaks
that clothed the island and chanced upon a clearing where newer
growth prevailed. There at the centre of the clearing stood an ancient
oak tree from which dangled an old ship's tackle block suspended from
a lopped-off limb some sixteen feet above the ground. A bowl-shaped
depression directly underneath suggested that the soil had sunk where
someone had buried something in the distant past. According to some
accounts the bark of the tree was heavily scored by rope marks.

The story of the tackle block is generally considered as an addition
to the tale of the discovery, it being argued that no one who had buried
something of value would be foolhardy enough to leave such evidence of
his work. However, there is the alternative suggestion that the tackle block

was left in such an obvious position in order to attract the attention of any who chanced that way, as one day they must. This implies that the tackle block, if it existed, might be interpreted as bait. Bait or not, the imagination of McGinnis was sufficiently stirred for him to return the following day with two companions, John Smith and Anthony Vaughan. The three young men must have been feverishly excited about their prospects.

It is reported that when they began to dig, they found themselves in a previously dug pit of circular shape, the diameter of which has been variously reported as between seven and sixteen feet, but the generally accepted dimension is thirteen feet. At a depth of two feet they unearthed a layer of flagstones, which were later thought to have originated from Gold River a couple of miles to the north. The soil within the pit was loose, and the hard clay walls were indented by the marks of tools used by previous diggers. At ten feet they came across a platform of oak logs that extended across the pit, the ends of which were securely embedded in the walls. The logs were rotten on the outside, suggesting that they had been buried for many years. A two-foot gap was encountered below the oak log platform indicating that the logs still had enough strength, and were sufficiently embedded in the hard natural ground, to support the weight of ten feet of earth.

Conditions below the first platform of logs have been described differently in the various references, and there is some uncertainty regarding the actual depth reached by the three pals before they relinquished their assault upon what later became known as the Money Pit. The *Liverpool Transcript* of October 16, 1862, printed a letter by J.B. McCully, which indicated that "a layer of oak timber" was found at ten feet, twenty feet and thirty feet, at which depth the work was stopped. The *Colonist* of January 2, 1864, indicated that McGinnis and his chums encountered an oak platform at ten feet and then extended the excavation fifteen feet below the platform, which suggests they stopped digging at a depth of twenty-five feet without finding additional oak log platforms. It is assumed that McCully's letter of 1862 reflects conditions encountered in that first digging of 1795. In any event, the group gave up the search and some nine years were to elapse before the Money Pit was excavated to greater depth.

Prior to the discovery, Oak Island had been surveyed by John Marshall in 1764 and subdivided into thirty-two lots of four acres each. The subsequent award of lots by draw and sale of lots started in the late 1760s and involved many parties. Extensive research on lot ownership prior to 1795 has been done by Paul Wroclawski and the interested reader is referred to his work. Figure 3 shows the location of the original lots on the island in relation to the Money Pit, as well as a notation of the present ownership. It should be noted that various name changes have been made to some of the island's features in recent times. Figure 4 shows the original topography at the east end of the island in contours of feet above mean sea level.

About eight years after the first diggings, the existence of the Money Pit was divulged to Simeon Lynds of Onslow, Nova Scotia, who was related to the Vaughan family. He formed a syndicate of friends, some of them locally well-known men, who were prepared to invest money in what became known as the Onslow Syndicate. Excavation work recommenced in 1804. An account of the work is documented in the *Colonist* of January 2, 1864, though it should be noted that there is an implied discrepancy regarding the year in which work was resumed. The article states that work was resumed fifteen years after the first discovery, making start of work in 1810, but other reports give 1804. This discrepancy is not considered important, and the year 1804 has been accepted as the start of the Onslow Syndicate search.

It is unfortunate that there is not a more detailed account of the findings of the Onslow Syndicate than that given in the newspapers, particularly with respect to the disposition of the oak platforms. Most writings since the 1950s refer to the finding of oak platforms at uniform intervals of ten feet to a depth of ninety feet. However, the earliest accounts make no mention of platforms being present below a depth of thirty feet. These same accounts do, however, refer to layers of charcoal, putty and coconut fibre being found at specific levels and a "mark

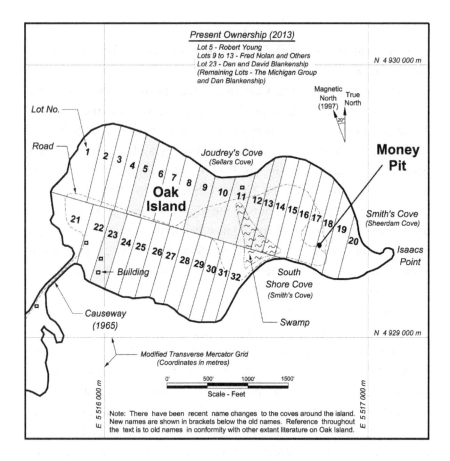

Figure 3

Oak Island Showing Original Lot Locations and Present Ownership

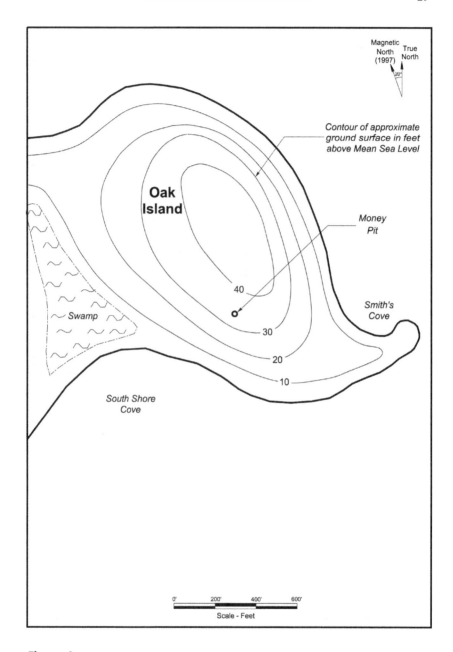

Figure 4

East End of Oak Island Showing Approximate Original Ground Surface
Contours

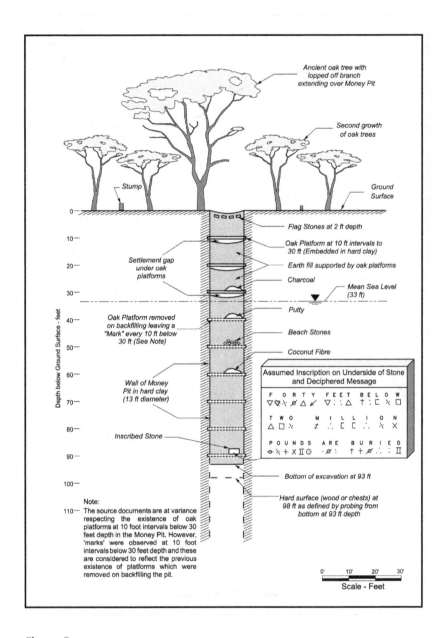

Figure 5

Reconstructed Section of Money Pit Based on Findings of Onslow Syndicate to 1804

every ten feet." This suggests that platforms had once existed below thirty feet but had been removed prior to backfilling the pit, the marks of their embedment remaining in the sides of the pit. The syndicate penetrated to a final depth of ninety-three feet. Figure 5 represents a reconstructed section through the Money Pit as interpreted from the reports arising from the work.

One of the interesting features of the Money Pit is the platforms inferred from the marks at ten-foot intervals. It is very likely that temporary platforms were installed at ten-foot intervals during the first digging. Figure 6 gives a speculative configuration that may have been used during excavation by the original workers. This would enable access of men and materials to be effected and would ensure earth support measures could be implemented as required. In the hard clay through which the pit was excavated little, if any, wall support was necessary. If the original diggers of the Money Pit were seafarers, removal of spoil and any water encountered would have been by windlass.

James McNutt, who was employed on the island in 1863, after the Onslow Syndicate had abandoned the site, wrote an account that differs from others. He mentions, "at forty feet a tier of charcoal; at fifty feet a tier of smooth stones from the beach, with figures and letters cut on them; at sixty feet a tier of manilla grass and the rind of a coconut; at seventy feet a tier of putty." The discrepancies in the various reports make it difficult to methodically interpret the early excavation activities on Oak Island.

The underground workings at Oak Island were almost certainly executed in two phases, each of which was carried out by separate groups at different periods of time. Therefore the charcoal, putty, beach stones and coconut fibre found at the various levels depicted on Figure 5 were more probably utilised during the second phase of the work. Since all these materials were encountered at specific levels, it must be concluded that they were left at these levels during the backfilling of the pit and during removal of the lower oak log platforms. Each of the materials encountered provides a clue to the history of the Money Pit and is worthy of comment.

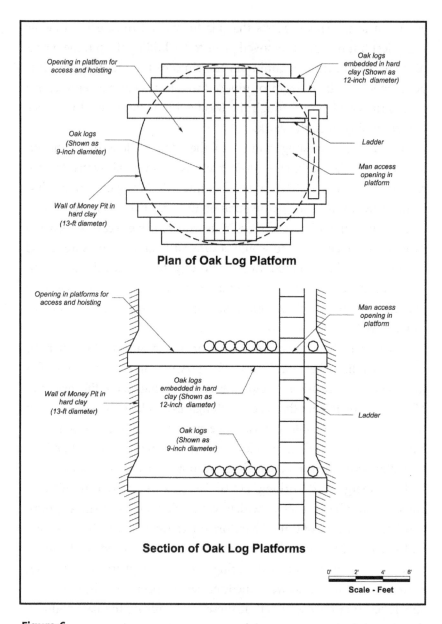

Figure 6

Speculated Configuration of Oak Log Platforms Used in the Original
Excavation of the Money Pit

Charcoal can be used for a number of purposes, including purifica-
tion of water on board ships, as an ingredient of gunpowder and as a
smokeless fuel. Its presence at a depth of thirty feet is meaningful. The
preeminent obstacle faced by underground workers is the provision of
fresh air in which to carry out their onerous work. In the seventeenth
century the practice of using furnaces to induce convection currents
of fresh air to ventilate underground workings began to be adopted.
This method was initiated in the coal mines around Liège, originally
in the Netherlands, but now in Belgium. The first written report about
it is contained in the *Philosophical Transactions of The Royal Society
of London*, after a lecture by Sir Robert Moray in July 1665. Figure 7
shows how this method of ventilating tunnels and shafts was applied.
Sir Robert describes the concept eloquently:

> At the mouth or entry of the Adit there is a structure
> raised of Brick, like a Chimney, some 28 or 30 foot high
> in all.... Then, some 3 foot above ground or more, there is
> on that side, that is next to the Adit or Pit, a square hole
> of 8 or 9 inches every way, by which the air enters to make
> the Fire burn. Into this hole there is fixed a square Tube
> or Pipe of Wood, whereof the Joints and Chinks are so
> stopt with Parchment pasted or glewed upon them, that
> the air can no where get in to the Pipe but at the end...
> and so, while the Air is drawn by the fire from the farthest
> or most inward part of the Mine or Adit, fresh Air must
> needs come in from without, to supply the place of the
> other, which by its motion doth carry away with it all the
> vapors, that breath out of the ground, by which means the
> whole Adit will be always filled with fresh air, so that men
> will there breath as surely as abroad, and not only candles
> burn, but Fire, when upon occasion there is use for it for
> breaking of the Rock.

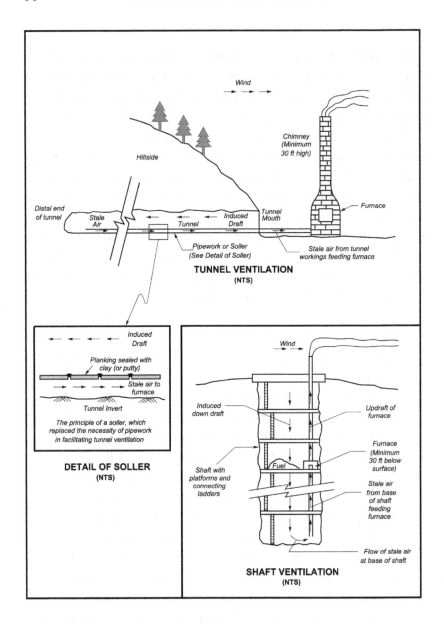

Figure 7

The Use of Furnaces in Ventilating Tunnels and Shafts

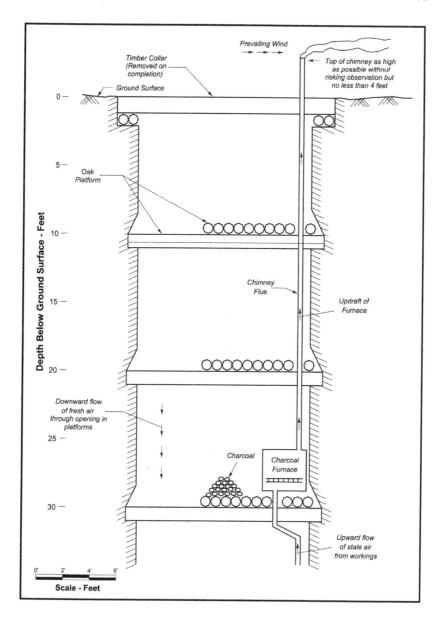

Figure 8

Cross-section Illustrating Concept for Ventilation of Money Pit with Charcoal Furnace

In the latter part of the seventeenth century and the early part of the eighteenth century, the ventilation practice described above was adopted universally throughout Europe, before eventually being superseded. Prior to Sir Robert Moray's discourse, the authoritative work on all aspects of mining was *De Re Metallica* by Georgius Agricola (1556). Since Agricola makes no mention of the use of furnaces for ventilation purposes, it may be concluded that some, if not all, of the Money Pit workings were excavated after the Liège practice became better known. Since a flue pipe needs to be at least thirty feet long to ensure an efficient draw, the finding of charcoal at this depth suggests that ventilation of the underground works at Oak Island was carried out by installing a furnace at a depth thirty feet below surface within the shaft. This approach would have allowed concealment of most of the chimney. Figure 8 gives a cross-section through the Money Pit illustrating how this feature was likely incorporated. Also, it is of interest to record that the use of furnaces to ventilate shafts and tunnels associated with placement of explosives during siege warfare was a common practice in the seventeenth century. This practice is described in detail by Christopher Duffy in his book *Fire and Stone: The Science of Fortress Warfare 1660–1860*.

Putty was reported at the forty-foot level. There was so much of it that twenty houses in Mahone Bay and the surrounding area used it for glazing windows. Putty is an excellent caulking material and, although entirely unsuitable for caulking seams on board ship (where flexure and movement is continual), its presence in the Money Pit is suggestive of its use in the sealing of sollers (see Figure 7) as well as a possible leakage problem.

The most likely use of beach stones was for backfilling the Flood Tunnel and possibly to give body to a caulking medium of putty and coconut fibre.

Many bushels of coconut fibre are reported to have been removed from the pit. This implies its use as a caulking medium alone, or in conjunction with putty. Coconut fibre has some interesting applications. It was once used for making ropes, and ropes from this fibre are still made in parts of the Orient. Though weaker than many traditional materials, such as hemp and sisal, it possesses the greatest resistance to decay in salt water and considerable elasticity. A four-inch diameter rope made from coconut fibre can reduce to a diameter of one inch under strain, with commensurate elongation. For this property, coconut fibre ropes were especially favoured as 'hurricane springs' enabling a ship to ride out a storm with less risk of losing cable or anchorage, provided of course there was adequate sea room. Coconut fibre is also a common packing material.

As the excavation of the Onslow Syndicate advanced through the original backfill in 1804, a large stone slab was encountered at a depth of ninety feet. It is reported that an inscription was found on the underside consisting of "a number of rudely cut letters and figures... they could not decipher it, as it was either too badly cut or did not appear to be in their own vernacular." From what we know, the dimensions of the stone were thirty-six by fifteen inches, and ten inches thick. A stone of this size would weigh about five hundred pounds. The dimensions vary according to the source of the account and smaller dimensions have been reported. One statement suggests the stone to have weighed about 175 pounds; another that it was freestone, the corners not squared, with the appearance of dark Swedish granite or porphyry, very hard with an olive tinge.

The stone had a very chequered career before its final disappearance sometime in the 1930s. After its recovery from the Money Pit, it was incorporated into John Smith's fireplace at his home on Oak Island, from which it was transferred to Halifax. It was reported that the stone "was taken to Halifax where they tried to decipher what was cut on it, but it had become so defaced it was illegible." In 1864 the stone was placed in the window of a bookbinder, A&H Creighton of 64 Upper Water Street, Halifax. Many recent publications include a facsimile of the inscription, but its origin and accuracy are likely beyond confirmation. The assumed inscription was not particularly difficult to decipher. It read "FORTY FEET BELOW TWO MILLION POUNDS

ARE BURIED" (see Figure 5). The present decimal system of coinage was adopted by Canada in 1871 so the term 'pounds' would have been current at the time of deciphering the stone. The interpretation of the inscription on Figure 5 shows the elementary nature of the cipher.

In addition, it is difficult to reconcile five points regarding this stone. Firstly, if the stone did really possess these cryptic markings, why did John Smith have such little regard for it and build it into his fireplace? Surely it would have deserved greater respect! Secondly, why do we first hear of the deciphered message at a time when Creighton, who was treasurer of the Oak Island Association (a subsequent treasure-seeking company), was attempting to raise funds for further excavation work by selling shares in the enterprise to the public? Thirdly, evidence of treasure was subsequently found at ten to fifteen feet below the inscribed stone and later at sixty-three to seventy feet below the stone. The forty-foot depth inscribed on the stone would appear erroneous. Fourthly, if the stone was intended to portray a cryptic message, why was the message on the underside of the stone? Fifthly, why would anyone concealing treasure of immense value bother to provide such a cryptic clue at the site? It is certain that the stone existed, and that it was recovered from the Money Pit, but the markings, to the extent that they actually existed, must be discounted as representing a clue to the contents of the Money Pit.

The reported physical features of the inscribed stone are consistent with the geological history of the area. Oak Island and its immediate environs are covered by a mantle of glacial drift that invaded the region from the northwest, the direction from which the latest glacial advance originated. Included within the drift are numerous glacial erratics, which are large boulders that were plucked from the bedrock by the immense thickness of ice that scoured the region. The Chester area, including Oak Island, is strewn with these erratics. Most of them are of granite, but some are of basalt, originating from North Mountain on the Bay of Fundy. This latter type of rock is dark coloured and on weathering adopts a dun-coloured hue. It is possible that the mysterious stone is nothing more than an erratic of basaltic composition that was encountered in the Money Pit by the original excavators, and being too heavy to remove was levered out of the way and left on one of the platforms. The crude markings on the stone could have been the handiwork of a fanciful workman, after which the stone was rolled over, out of the way.

The excavation in the Money Pit proceeded below ninety feet, and water problems began to be experienced as a depth of ninety-three feet was reached, with one cask of water being raised for every two of moist earth. Probing ahead with an iron bar, the syndicate encountered a hard, resistant surface at ninety-eight feet that appeared to extend across the entire width of the shaft. The *Colonist* of January 2, 1864, reported that "some supposed it was wood, and others a chest." The treasure-seekers must have been elated by the looming prospects of untold wealth. Since it was Saturday, work was not resumed until the following Monday. The fury and chagrin of the diggers can be imagined when on their return they found the Money Pit full of water to sea level, thirty-three feet below ground surface.

Attempts were made to bail out the water. However, equipped with only the simplest contrivances, it was impossible for the diggers to make meaningful headway. A pump was obtained but promptly burst, being unable to cope with the head of water. As 1804 drew to its close, work was postponed in order to rethink the situation.

In 1805 the syndicate attempted to get at the treasure, which they were convinced lay just beyond their grasp, by excavating a shaft adjacent to the Money Pit. This shaft (Shaft No. 2) was located approximately fourteen feet to the southeast (or east). The digging was more tedious as this time the diggers were excavating through hard virgin ground rather than cleaning out loose spoil from an infilled shaft. Despite the toughness of the soil, they reached a depth of 110 feet without any insurmountable problems, and little ingress of water. Then, approximately ten feet below the imagined treasure they began to dig sideways towards the Money Pit with the objective of recovering the

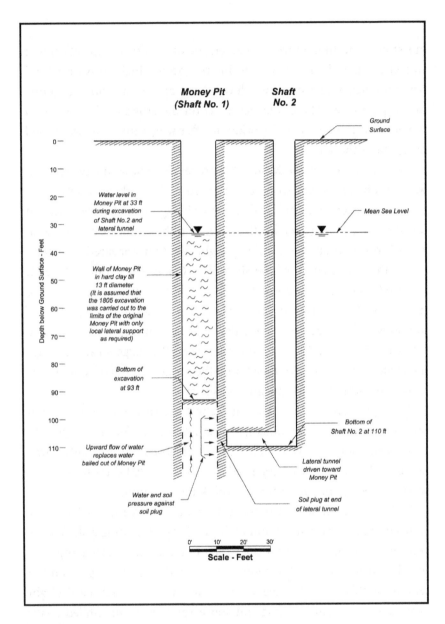

Figure 9

Section Through Money Pit and Shaft No. 2 in 1805 Before Tunnel Failure and Shaft Flooding

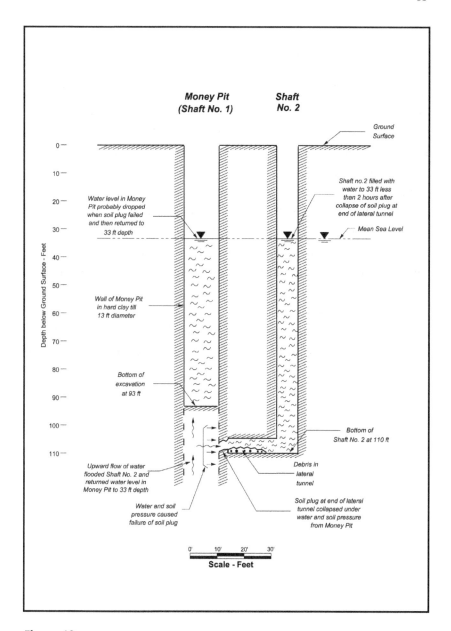

Figure 10

Section Through Money Pit and Shaft No. 2 in 1805 After Tunnel Failure and Shaft Flooding

treasure from below (see Figure 9). When the tunnel they had dug was within about two feet of the closest side to the Money Pit, water started to break through and finally the face burst (see Figure 10). Water and debris poured in to flood out all their work. Those below ground at the time were lucky to escape with their lives. In less than two hours the water level rose in the new shaft to a level identical to that in the Money Pit itself.

Figures 9 and 10 show the conditions before and after the failure, and how the soil plug between the tunnel and shaft collapsed due to pressure from the water column in the Money Pit. The source of the water that flowed into Shaft No. 2 was the water column in the Money Pit. It would be verified during subsequent shaft excavations by the Halifax Company in 1867 that another source of flood water lay deep within the Money Pit.

The year 1805 closed in much frustration. The Onslow Syndicate did not return, and it was forty years before another group of adventurers tried their luck.

CHAPTER 2
The Treasure Proves Elusive

Turn, Fortune, turn thy wheel with smile or frown.
"Fortune" (Tennyson)

In 1845 a new company recommenced the search for treasure on Oak Island. No doubt McGinnis, Smith, Vaughan and possibly others carried out some probings of their own on the island in the intervening years, but there is nothing to suggest that such probings were fruitful. By 1845 McGinnis was out of the picture, and Smith, though continuing to reside on the island and affirming his belief that treasure was buried there, remained aloof from the new venture. Only Vaughan involved himself, and he was then sixty-three years of age.

The new syndicate, known as the Truro Syndicate, included Dr. David Barnes Lynds (a relative of the Simeon Lynds who had been a member of the earlier Onslow Syndicate), John Gammell, Adams A. Tupper and Robert Creelman. The excavation work was to be supervised by Jotham McCully (manager) and James Pitblado (foreman).

Active work commenced in 1849. The original Money Pit shaft (Shaft No. 1) and the adjacent Shaft No. 2 had collapsed, forming a single 'glory hole' full of water and debris. The hole was cleaned out and after a mere twelve days of hard work, the venturers had reached a depth of eighty-six feet. No mention was made of any oak platforms being encountered during this activity and it must be assumed that any platforms (where they existed) had been removed by the Onslow Syndicate.

Though the Truro Syndicate managed to reach a depth of eighty-six feet without experiencing any problems with inflows of water, this favourable state of affairs did not persist. The *Colonist* of January 7, 1864, reporting on the excavation some fifteen years later, states:

Sabbath morning came and no sign of water, more than usual appearing in the Pit, the men left for church in Chester Village with lighter hearts. At two o'clock they returned from church, and to their great surprise found water standing in the Pit, to the depth of sixty feet, being on a level with that in the Bay.

Attempts to bail out the water, or to make serious inroads into controlling the inflow, were fruitless. The men resorted to probing the depths with a pod-auger working from a platform erected at a depth of thirty feet. Five holes were put down to depths ranging from 106 to 112 feet (from ground surface). The first two holes encountered mud and stones, but the next three produced exciting prospects of wealth, tantalisingly just beyond their grasp. McCully's later statement included the following:

The platform (found in the Pit in 1804) was struck at 98 feet just as the old diggers found it, when sounding with the iron bar. After going through the platform, which was five inches thick, and proved to be spruce, the auger dropped twelve inches and then went through four inches of oak; then it went through twenty-two inches of metal in pieces; but the auger failed to bring up anything in the nature of treasure, except three links of an ancient watch chain. It then went through eight inches of oak, which was thought to be the bottom of the first box and the top of the next; then twenty-two inches of metal, the same as before; then four inches of oak and six inches of spruce, then into clay seven feet without striking anything.

It was also reported that in the fourth hole several splinters of oak and birch were recovered, suggesting the presence of casks, as well as what appeared to be coconut fibre. The results were described by McCully in the following terms:

The platform was struck, as before, at 98 feet; passing through this, the auger fell about 18 inches and came in contact with (as supposed) the side of a cask. The flat chisel revolving close to the side of the cask gave it a jerky and irregular motion. On withdrawing the auger, several splinters of oak (believed to be from the bulge of a cask) such as might come from the side of an oak stave, a piece of hoop made of birch and a small quantity of brown fibrous substance, closely resembling the husk of a coconut, were brought up.

The findings inferred from the 1849 drilling program are illustrated schematically in Figure 11, with upper and lower platforms enclosing the assumed chests and casks filled with treasure.

The borings were of immense importance to the treasure-seekers. Not only did the results give some tangible evidence that there was indeed treasure buried within the Money Pit, establishing with reasonable certainty the existence of chests, casks or wooden boxes contained between platforms at 98 and 105 feet below ground surface, but they also gave new heart to the diggers' endeavours. There may have been some exaggeration with respect to the "three links of watch chain," as James McNutt, writing in 1867, refers to the discovery of three pieces of copper wire. However, McNutt adds that grass, the same as encountered at sixty feet, was recovered, together with a substance resembling putty.

During the drilling of the fifth hole an incident occurred that heightened the tension on the site. James Pitblado, the foreman, was scrutinizing each fragment being brought to the surface. There is a story that he secreted upon his person something that he recovered from the auger. Though challenged at the time, Pitblado said he would show it to the directors at the next meeting. This is strange, as those directors were on site in person. Pitblado never attended that meeting. He left the island and soon after, he and a friend (Charles Dickson

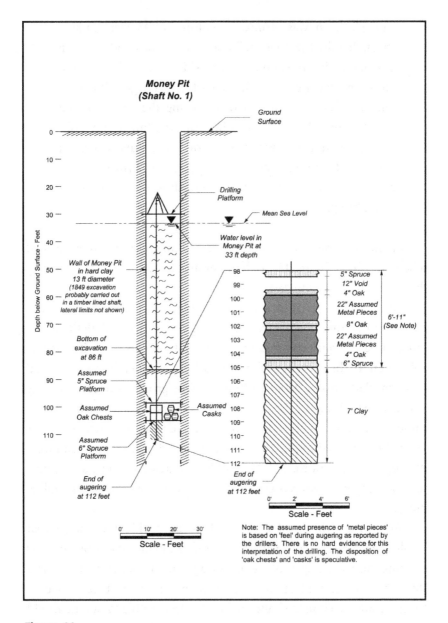

Figure 11

Results of Auger Drilling by Truro Syndicate in 1849

Archibald, manager of the Acadian Iron Works at Londonderry, Nova Scotia), attempted to buy the east end of the island from John Smith. The actions of Pitblado strongly suggest that something of value was indeed recovered from the end of the auger, but what it was will never be known. Pitblado was reported to have died in a gold mine accident some months later.

In 1850, a new shaft (Shaft No. 3) was commenced slightly to the northwest (or west) of the Money Pit and about ten feet away from it. They dug to a depth of 109 feet and tried to gain access to the treasure by approaching it from below. They experienced the same type of failure as their predecessors, water and debris bursting into the shaft with the men barely escaping with their lives. This time the water rose somewhat slower in the new shaft but eventually attained sea level. Though their efforts met with unmitigated failure, some new evidence emerged. A workman fell into the shaft and, through this salutary experience, learned that the water was salty. It is surprising that this fact had not emerged earlier from all the bailing that had been carried out. It was also discovered that the water levels in the open shafts rose and fell in direct relation to the tides.

The lessons learned from their failures suggested to the Truro Syndicate that a man-made flooding system existed, one that was intended to frustrate the recovery of any treasure buried within the Money Pit. An intense search along the shorelines revealed a length of beach at Smith's Cove worthy of closer examination, and a stunning discovery was made. Observations had disclosed that, for a length of about 145 feet, the shingle on the beach oozed water more than else-where when the tide was on the ebb. Also boulders appeared to have been removed to the two extremities. Some frenzied digging took place, and within a few hours a cunning filter system had been uncovered.

The filter system exposed in 1850 has been described in many sourc-es, and one of the more complete descriptions is given in the affidavit of Adams A. Tupper, included in the booklet titled *The Oak Island Story* published in 1895. Mr. Tupper was present during the work and his affidavit reports:

After removing the sand and gravel covering the beach, they came to a covering or bed of a brown, fibrous plant, the fibre very much resembling the husk of a cocoanut.... The surface covered by this plant extended 145 feet along the shoreline, and from a little above low to high water mark, and about 2 inches in thickness. Underlying this and to the same extent was about 4 or 5 inches of decayed eel grass, and under this was a compact mass of beach rocks free from sand and gravel.

In order to further investigate the filter system, an earth cofferdam was constructed to isolate the 145-foot wide beach area from the sea. The water within the cofferdam was pumped out and further digging revealed a unique system of drains that were described by Tupper as follows:

After removing the rocks nearest the low water, it was found that the clay (which with the sand and gravel originally formed the beach) had been dug out and removed and replaced by beach rocks. Resting on the bottom of this excavation were five well constructed drains (as shown on the plan) formed by laying parallel lines of rocks about 8 inches apart and covering the same with flat stones. These drains at the starting point were a considerable distance apart, but converged towards a common centre at the back of the excavation. With the exception of these drains the other rocks had evidently been thrown in promiscuously. Work went on until half the rocks had been removed where the clay banks at the extreme sides showed a depth of 5 ft., at which depth a partially burned piece of oak wood was found.

The drains at the base of the filter bed were reported as sloping downward toward a presumed vertical shaft or cistern somewhat inland of the high water mark. In the belief that the water intake system they had found fed a tunnel linking Smith's Cove with the Money Pit, the Truro Syndicate excavated further inland in the direction where the drains led, in an attempt to locate a shaft or cistern. Because of the soft, waterlogged nature of the ground, this proved impracticable. Subsequent flooding of the area due to breaching of the cofferdam from unusually high tides caused abandonment of this line of exploration.

Sketches of the filter system, based on Tupper's description and a rough sketch given in *The Oak Island Story*, are shown on Figures 12 and 13. The filter bed of coconut fibre and eel grass above the drains was successful in preventing the drains from clogging through the ingress of silt and sand. The unique drainage system and the cunningness of the filter bed demonstrates the ability of the party responsible for the work to design and construct a water intake system to withstand the ravages of time. Today's engineers could not exhibit greater expertise.

An interesting point with regard to the original construction of the filter bed is that the average sea level at the time of the work would have been significantly lower than it is now. The relative sea level in Maritime Canada has been rising at a rate of about 0.75 to 1.0 feet per century over the past two thousand years. More specifically the rate of rise in the Halifax and Mahone Bay area has been about one foot per century. This is a comparatively high rate of relative sea level rise, which results from a combination of normal global sea level increase and land subsidence due to what is referred to in geological terms as 'collapse of the peripheral forebulge.' This latter component accounts for about half of the relative sea level rise at Mahone Bay. Figure 13 shows the previous average sea level in 1750, which is about 2.5 feet lower than current average sea level. Also shown is the typical seven-foot range of large tides for 1750. The relevance of this date will be discussed in later chapters.

After the excavation at Smith's Cove, the syndicate resorted to attempting to discover the line of the envisaged tunnel by sinking a number of shafts and exploring the region by tunnelling. The result was a confusing array of shafts and tunnels in the region, the locations

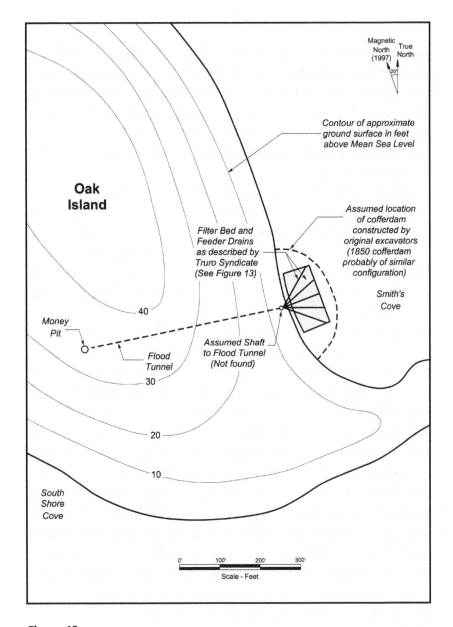

Figure 12

Location of Filter Bed Discovered at Smith's Cove by Truro Syndicate in 1850

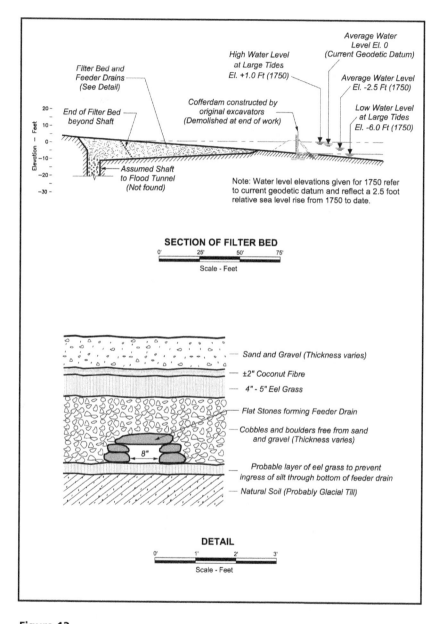

Figure 13

Section and Detail of Filter Bed at Smith's Cove Discovered by Truro
Syndicate in 1850

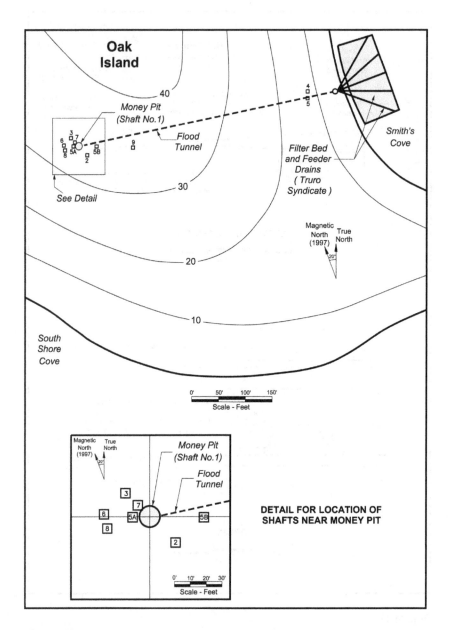

Figure 14

Location of Shafts Excavated to 1867

of which are uncertain. Despite this confusion, there is consistent reference to two shafts (numbers 4 and 5) in the written record. Though there is some variance of opinion regarding their exact location, it is reasonable to assume that they were near Smith's Cove (see Figure 14).

Shaft No. 4 was put down to a depth of seventy-five feet and encountered only the hard clayey soil of the island. Shaft No. 5 was put down some twelve feet to the south of No. 4. In most of the written accounts it is reported that a large boulder was encountered at a depth of thirty-five feet and, after it was pried up, the shaft immediately filled with sea water to tide level. The exception to these accounts is the one contained in the prospectus (1900) of the Oak Island Treasure Company, in which Shaft No. 5 was reported to have encountered water at a depth of eighty feet as a result of prying up a boulder at a location close to Smith's Cove. Despite these differences, it was obvious that a connection via tunnel had been found between Smith's Cove and the Money Pit. This connection became known as the Flood Tunnel and was of the order of five hundred feet long. An immense achievement by any standard of construction!

Though the line of the Flood Tunnel had been located, it was found impossible to cut off the flow of water to the Money Pit by driving spiles and heavy timbers in the bottom of Shaft No. 5. Once again the treasure-seekers had to retire to lick their wounds and think again.

At this point in the record of the activities of the Truro Syndicate (1850), a major collapse of the Money Pit was apparently experienced when the syndicate resorted to excavating another shaft immediately adjacent to it. However, later researchers concluded that the collapse occurred in 1861 during the digging of the next group of treasure-seekers. This latter viewpoint is substantiated by "the digger Patrick" in the *Novascotian* dated September 30, 1861.

In deference to "the digger Patrick," the major collapse of the Money Pit mentioned above is credited to the activities of the Oak Island Association, the successor to the Truro Syndicate, when they dug Shaft

No. 6 (as described later). However, before that inauspicious event, the Truro Syndicate was to experience a virtual repeat of the disaster that had struck them only a few months earlier. They excavated Shaft No. 5A, slightly west of the Money Pit, to a depth of 112 feet. Once again the hard, clayey soil of the island was dug without incident. Then they drove a tunnel towards the Money Pit and, yet again, had to flee for their lives as water and debris burst into the workings. With their funds exhausted, the Truro Syndicate abandoned Oak Island, and nine years were to elapse before another Truro-based group attempted to match their wits against the Money Pit.

A number of independent attempts were made to search for treasure on the island between 1850 and 1860. John Smith passed away in 1857 and his property was taken over by an Anthony Graves who built a house and farmed the east end of the island. During his residence on the island, Graves is reputed to have purchased supplies in the Mahone Bay area with Spanish coins, and when his house was torn down in 1930, Spanish coins dated 1785 were found. Since this date is subsequent to the signing of the Shoreham Grant, and only precedes the finding of the Money Pit by ten years, it is unlikely that there is any connection between Graves's secret store of wealth and the Money Pit.

In 1859 the Truro Syndicate regrouped and resumed excavation using steam-operated pumps to dewater the Money Pit. However, the pumps failed and the water stubbornly remained within the pit. Various theories were propounded on the assumption that the Flood Tunnel might be the means of entering the Money Pit beneath the treasure and that control gates to hold back the water were situated somewhere along the route of the tunnel. Such theories were little more than wild speculation.

In 1860, yet another Truro-based syndicate was formed, identifying itself as the Oak Island Association. This group included Adams A. Tupper, Jotham McCully and James McNutt from the previous syndicate, with a new investor named Jefferson McDonald. Work commenced in 1861 with the efforts directed at reinstating the Money Pit, which was cleaned out and recribbed to a depth of eighty-eight feet. This was achieved without experiencing major inflows of water into the shaft. However, the Oak Island Association was reluctant to make a frontal assault on the Money Pit by deepening it below this level. Instead they dug Shaft No. 5B at a location twenty-five feet east of the Money Pit in the hopes of intercepting the Flood Tunnel believed to link the Money Pit with Smith's Cove. The shaft was dug to 120 feet without locating any man-made excavations and was abandoned. Another shaft (Shaft No. 6) was put down eighteen feet west (or south) of the Money Pit and advanced to 118 feet. Again a tunnel was driven from the bottom of the shaft towards the Money Pit, and again the tunnel was inundated with water and mud. This was the fourth attempt to penetrate the Money Pit using this technique, and the fourth calamity!

A strenuous effort was made to bail out the Money Pit and the adjacent shafts. Over a period of several days, using the efforts of sixty-three men and thirty-three horses, the water in Shaft No. 6 was lowered sufficiently to enable men to enter the lateral tunnel at the bottom of the shaft, at a depth of 118 feet. A thunderous crash was heard and the men in the shaft barely escaped from being drowned in a rush of mud and water that engulfed the works. Desperate bailing continued over a period of several days and the water level was lowered, then a second thunderous crash was heard. This was followed by the collapse of the new timbering within the Money Pit itself, with only the upper thirty feet remaining intact. After the collapse, the bottom was sounded at a depth of 102 feet when previously the bottom had been at eighty-eight feet, fourteen feet higher. It was speculated that the first crash to be heard represented the collapse of the lower platform at 105 feet, which supported the treasure, and that the second crash represented the collapse of the upper platform at ninety-eight feet.

Following the collapse of the timbering, there was considerable speculation on how far the treasure chests may have dropped. Some opinions suggested they may have disappeared into a massive void;

other more realistic opinions suggested about fouteen feet, the drop determined from sounding. Regardless of these opinions, some positive aspects of the disaster became manifest. Certain artifacts were recovered from the inrush of mud, water and debris that had engulfed the adjacent Shaft No. 6. These are recorded as having included a piece of juniper with bark intact (cut with an edged tool), a piece of oak three feet long and six inches in diameter, a slab of spruce with a bored hole (the bored hole possibly originating from the 1849 augering operations), the end of a cask and quantities of coconut fibre.

In the fall of 1861 the Oak Island Association, undaunted by the earlier collapse, set up a cast iron pump and steam engine to facilitate dewatering. Shortly after pumping commenced, the boiler burst, scalding one man to death. This was the first fatality experienced since digging started in 1795.

The following year (1862), the Oak Island Association resorted to the same plan so unsuccessfully adopted by their predecessors: they sank Shaft No. 7 close to the Money Pit on its western side. They excavated to a depth of 107 feet and used this as a pumping shaft for the steam driven pump. The Money Pit was then reinstated to a depth of 103 feet but it could not be deepened any further as the water persisted at this level. During this work they encountered tools abandoned by the Onslow and Truro groups in 1804 and 1850 respectively. Undeterred by their inability to excavate deeper, they commenced Shaft No. 8. This shaft was located close to Shaft No. 6 (see Figure 14). At the same time they again turned their attention to Smith's Cove and attempted to cut off the supply of water to the Money Pit by sealing the filter bed with clay.

The degree to which the efforts at Smith's Cove were effective is not known, and no records exist as to the fate of Shaft No. 8, the final depth reached or the reason for abandonment. Resolutely, work began on Shaft No. 9 located about one-hundred feet to the east of the Money Pit, and twenty feet south of the presumed straight-line route of the Flood Tunnel.

At a depth of 120 feet, several horizontal tunnels were dug in an attempt to locate the Flood Tunnel. This must have been a hazardous undertaking in view of previous experiences. One of these exploration tunnels is reported as entering the Money Pit at a level of 108 feet, the Flood Tunnel itself not being encountered. According to the records, the operators were successful in pumping the Money Pit dry to this level. J.B. Leedham, in charge of the site operations, descended to this depth and noted that on one side of the Money Pit the walls were hard, but exceptionally soft elsewhere, so soft that a crowbar could be sunk into the soil quite effortlessly. From all accounts another tunnel was run from the 108-foot level in the Money Pit to Shaft No. 2, which had been sunk in 1805. No evidence was found to indicate the fate of any treasure chests following the collapse of the Money Pit in 1861.

Funds to finance further excavation work began to run dry about this time, and in March 1866 the directors ceded their rights on the island to the Oak Island Eldorado Company, later known as the Halifax Company. Rumours circulated that the directors, prior to ceding their rights to the Halifax Company, returned to the site clandestinely and removed the treasure. The truth of such rumours will never be known, but it is certain that none of the directors ever flaunted any wealth in later years.

CHAPTER 3

A Flood Tunnel is Confirmed

Full many a gem of purest ray serene,
The dark unfathomed caves of ocean bear
"Elegy in a Country Churchyard" (Gray)

Not a great deal of useful information was volunteered by the Halifax Company regarding their operations. Apparently they did extensive exploratory tunnelling, but few records survive. This lack of reliable information led in later years to various assumptions being made regarding the origin of certain tunnels. It was assumed that these tunnels were dug by the Halifax Company, but they might have been dug long before the Money Pit was discovered in 1795.

In 1866, the first endeavour of the Halifax Company was to construct a cofferdam around the inlet works to the Flood Tunnel at Smith's Cove. The objective, as described in their prospectus (quoted from *The Oak Island Mystery* by R.V. Harris), was:

> to build a substantial wood and clay dam seaward to extend out and beyond the rock work, so as to encompass the whole [cove?] within the dam [and] to pump out all the water within the area, and so block up the inlet from the sea.

S.C. Fraser, foreman for the Halifax Company, reported that this cofferdam was twelve feet high, 375 feet long and extended 120 feet offshore from the high-water mark. Though it operated successfully for a period after dewatering was achieved, it was destroyed by sea action before the area could be fully explored. However, timbers were recovered from the area of the cofferdam by John Wonnaccott in January 2004 and were subject to dendrochronology examination, the science of dating trees from the tree ring count, as well as carbon dating. The tree ring count approach was inclusive but the carbon dating results were consistent with the period of the work by the Halifax Company.

Following abandonment of exploration at Smith's Cove, the company resorted to the same plan as their predecessors: they re-excavated the Money Pit. Aided by pumps, they managed to clean it out to 108 feet, just five feet below the depth reached by the Oak Island Association four years earlier. While excavating a lateral tunnel into the south side of the pit, a workman named Robinson felt the ground give way beneath him. He drove his pick and crowbar into the ground and detected a cavity beneath his feet before escaping as water began to flood the tunnel. The water entered the workings so fast that it could not be controlled by the available pumps.

The Halifax Company elected to carry out some drilling in an attempt to locate the assumed chests and casks of treasure that had fallen deeper into the Money Pit after its collapse in 1861. They erected a platform at the ninety-foot level and began to drill through a three-inch pipe. The drilling spanned the period November 1866 to January 1867. As far as the evidence of treasure was concerned, the results proved disappointing, however the findings were of value. The boreholes penetrated to a maximum depth of 163 feet. They encountered spruce wood at 106 feet, coarse gravel and soft clay to 122 feet, soft clay with less gravel to 125 feet, at which depth they recovered more wood, charcoal and some coconut fibre. At 134 feet more wood and coconut fibre was recovered, the wood being in the form of oak chips, and a plank appears to have been penetrated. Intermittent loss of wash-water used in the drilling operation was reported, suggesting that a number of voids were being penetrated. At 158 feet a reddish-brown soil was encountered, the nature of which was not enlarged upon. In the upper part of the boreholes, the presence of voids entrapped within irregularly spaced timbers in association with fragments of charcoal, coconut fibre and a generous amount of soft clay mixed with coarse gravel suggests that debris from the collapse was being penetrated. An interesting fact emerging from this drilling was that no regular spacing of timber platforms was encountered. This is consistent with the absence of timber platforms at ten-foot intervals from forty to ninety feet, as inferred earlier, although the "marks" of such platforms were found.

The Halifax Company commenced Shaft No. 10, about two hundred feet southeast of the Money Pit and approximately 175 feet south of the estimated route of the Flood Tunnel. The shaft penetrated to a depth of about 110 feet. From the base of the shaft a number of exploratory tunnels were dug in an attempt to find the Flood Tunnel and divert its flow away from the Money Pit. They also extended tunnels towards the Money Pit. S.C. Fraser, the foreman on the site, describes vividly in his later writings of June 1895 the manner in which the Flood Tunnel was found:

> The Halifax Company's work was at a base of 110 feet, except two circling tunnels which were at a higher level.... As we entered the old place of the treasure (by a tunnel) we cut off the mouth of the 'pirate tunnel.' As we opened it the water hurled rocks about twice the size of a man's head, with many smaller, and drove the men back for protection. We could not go into the shaft (pit) again for about nine hours. Then the pumps conquered and we went down and cleared it out. The (pirate) tunnel was found near the top of our tunnel. I brought Mr. Hill, the engineer, down and he put his arm into the hole of the tunnel, up to his shoulder.... There was no mistake about our search in the old treasure place.

Fraser further describes the Flood Tunnel at its entrance to the Money Pit in a letter of June 19, 1895:

It was made of round stones, such as are found abundantly
on the beach and fields around the island. Where we found
it was the mouth of it, where it empties on to the treasure
before it, the treasure, went down.... We made no effort to
stop the flow of water from the drain, first we were at the
wrong end and again, with the pumps going, we could not.

Fraser's writings indicate his certainty that the Flood Tunnel was
encountered at the point where it entered the Money Pit, even though
this would have been about two-hundred feet from Shaft No. 10. Also,
Fraser's writings suggest that by pumping from the tunnel system
and from the Money Pit, which was reinstated to 108 feet, the Halifax
Company was able to successfully handle the flow from the Flood
Tunnel, even though the tunnel was linked directly to the sea. It is likely that the activities of the Truro Syndicate, in attempting to cut off the
water flow by spiling (1850), and those of the Oak Island Association,
in blanketing the inlet filter beds with clay (1862), contributed to this
accomplishment. A lower tidal range at the time might also have been
favourable. The Halifax Company confirmed the connection between
the Flood Tunnel at the Money Pit and the filter bed at Smith's Cove
by an experiment. During the pumping operation, clay was dumped at
the filter bed and about one-half hour later the water in the pit became
muddy.

It was reported by Fraser that the Flood Tunnel was filled with
rounded beach stones, similar to those found during the first excavations
within the Money Pit itself. The latter are likely to have been surplus to
tunnel backfilling. The Halifax Company reported that the Flood Tunnel
had dimensions of 2½ feet wide and 4 feet high, with an upward gradient
of 22½ degrees at its intersection with the Money Pit.

The internal dimensions of the tunnel may appear too small for
working with comfort. This may be so, but these measurements were
common during the two centuries prior to the discovery of the Money
Pit. Robert Hunt in his treatise *British Mining* (1884) states:

> In some of the old tin mines in Cornwall, and in a few of
> the ancient lead mines in the North and in Wales we find
> tunnels only three or four feet in height and only two and
> a half feet in width. In metallic mines at the present day the
> dimensions are six feet by five feet.

The British military of the eighteenth century used dimensions of
2½ feet wide by 4 feet high in much of their tunneling. Also small tunnels of the size referred to by Robert Hunt were used by sappers during World War I to set explosive charges below enemy trenches. An
account of their exceptional tunnelling accomplishments is described
in entertaining fashion by Alexander Barrie in his book titled *War
Underground: The Tunnellers of the Great War* and in a more recent
well-illustrated book by Barton, Doyle and Vandewalle titled *Beneath
Flanders Field: The Tunnellers' War 1914–18.*

Due to a lack of funds the Halifax Company discontinued its
operations in 1867 and no major works were to be carried out on Oak
Island until 1895. However, one particular incident occurred during
this interlude that is worthy of comment. This involved the discovery
of what has become known as the Cave-In Shaft. After John Smith
died in 1857, the eastern end of the island was taken over by Anthony
Graves, whose daughters Sophia and Rachel inherited the property
after his death in 1887. Sophia married Henry Sellers, and in 1878,
while ploughing with oxen on Lot 19, a "well-like" hole developed
beneath her team. The oxen were rescued, but in order to prevent any
such repetition of this event, her husband filled up the open hole with
boulders. The location of the cave-in was on a straight line between the
Money Pit and Smith's Cove, approximately 350 feet from the former
and 150 feet from the latter. The Cave-In Shaft was designated as Shaft
No. 11 and was re-excavated and explored at a later date.

A number of artifacts were found on the island following the work
by the Halifax Company. In 1885 a whistle made of bone or ivory was
found on the shore of Smith's Cove. Another whistle was found in

1901. There is no description of the former, but the latter is said to have been in the shape of a violin. Another discovery made subsequent to 1895 was that of a copper coin weighing 1½ ounces, which is variously reported to have borne the date 1317 or 1713. The latter seems more probable, and is significant as it was the year in which Acadia was ceded by France to Great Britain. None of these finds can be attributed to the construction of the Money Pit, but they testify to the presence of human beings on the island in the early part of the eighteenth century if the date of 1713 is a reliable one.

CHAPTER 4

The Clues Begin to Accumulate

Where Alph the sacred river, ran
Through caverns measureless to man
Down to a sunless sea

"Kubla Khan" (Coleridge)

Frederick Blair of Amherst, Nova Scotia, had been intrigued with the mystery of Oak Island since boyhood. Full of confidence, and brimming with enthusiasm, he was instrumental in forming the Oak Island Treasure Company in 1893, which retained some of the officers of the Halifax Company, including S.C. Fraser. The new company set itself the prime objective of cutting off the water supply to the Money Pit.

The first task undertaken in 1894 was to re-excavate the Cave-In Shaft (Shaft No. 11). The boulders used by Mr. Sellers to backfill the cave-in of 1878 were removed to a depth of fifteen feet, below which a well-defined circular shaft of six to eight feet diameter was found. This was cleaned out to fifty-five feet at which depth salt water was encountered and rose to a level corresponding to tide level, which could not be lowered by pumping. Since there had been no digging in this area by previous treasure-seekers, it was concluded that the shaft intersected the Flood Tunnel. As the ground surface at the Cave-In Shaft is twenty feet above mean sea level, the digging suggested that the Flood Tunnel at this location was at least thirty-five feet below sea level.

The next objective of the Oak Island Treasure Company was to locate the Flood Tunnel, undermine it and destroy it. To this end they dug Shaft No. 12, thirty feet east of the Money Pit at a point about eight feet north of the presumed Flood Tunnel alignment. At a depth of forty-three feet water burst into the shaft. Clearly this inflow was not directly from the Flood Tunnel itself and could have originated from a number of sources, such as the nearby Shaft No. 5B excavated in 1861 (see Figure 15), or an unknown tunnel put down by an earlier treasure-seeking group. In any event, after bailing out the water, work on the shaft continued to a final depth of fifty-five feet from which exploratory tunnels were driven in a southerly direction. The Flood Tunnel was not encountered, which seems reasonable since present-day knowledge indicates it must have been some forty to fifty feet lower.

Shaft No. 13 was then commenced about twenty-five feet north of the Cave-In Shaft (see Figure 15). At a depth of eighty-two feet tunnelling was commenced southwards in an attempt to strike the Flood Tunnel. After being flooded out initially, an old tunnel was encountered that was believed to have originated with the Halifax Company in 1867. The objective set by the company to locate the Flood Tunnel, undermine it and destroy it in order to enter the Money Pit had not been accomplished.

In 1895, under the direction of Adams A. Tupper, a mining engineer, the company decided to make a direct assault on the Money Pit. One of the last acts of the Halifax Company in 1867, twenty-eight years earlier, had been to construct a substantial platform within the pit at the thirty-foot level and to fill the pit to the surface. Unknowingly, Tupper started his excavation not at the Money Pit, but at Shaft No. 3 excavated by the Truro Syndicate in 1850, and located some ten feet to the northwest. This mistake was not realised until April 1897, after two years of much effort and expenditure to attain the 110-foot level. Extensive pumping was required in order to cope with heavy inflows of water at various levels, but finally at the base of the shaft an old tunnel was found that led to the Money Pit where "water was boiling up through the bottom."

The Money Pit shaft was then cleaned out and reinstated to a depth of 111 feet. The exit of the Flood Tunnel into the Money Pit was exposed, confirming the dimensions (2½ feet wide by 4 feet high) and

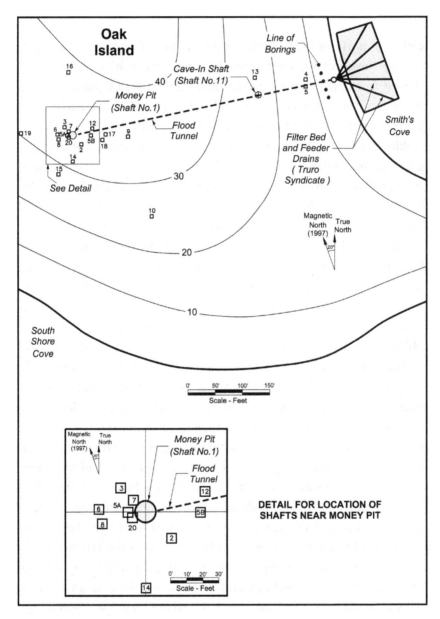

Figure 15

Location of Shafts Excavated to 1900

Photo 1 — Smith's Cove about 1897 with primeval forest oaks.

Photo 2 — Operations by the Oak Island Treasure Company in 1897.

infilling (smooth beach stones) reported by the Halifax Company in 1867. It is assumed that the top of the Flood Tunnel would have been at a depth of about 110 feet and that local excavation below 111 feet would have been carried out to define the bottom of the Flood Tunnel at 114 feet. Exposure of the Flood Tunnel resulted in a large increase in the rate of water entering the shaft, an increase that could not be handled by the available pumps. As a consequence, the water level in the Money Pit returned to tide level. There are some reports that pump failures occurred, contributing to this flooding. In any event, the work within the Money Pit came to a grinding halt in June 1897, but not before another fatality on March 26, 1897, when a man named Kaiser fell to his death after a hoist-rope broke.

In 1897 a water-diviner named Chapman, from Medford, Massachusetts, also visited Oak Island and mapped various tunnel positions. Some of the tunnels known to exist from the available records compared favourably with Chapman's predictions. He appears to have correctly predicted the intersection of the Flood Tunnel with the Money Pit at the 110-foot level without any prior knowledge of this important detail.

In the belief that the sole supply of water to the Money Pit came via the Flood Tunnel from Smith's Cove, an effort was made to cut off this supply in a more positive manner. Five borings were made at fifteen-foot spacings, which straddled the presumed tunnel alignment at a location about fifty feet inland from the high-water mark (see Figure 15). All borings were put down to between eighty and ninety-five foot depths. The central boring was the only one to intercept anything other than hard virgin ground. It struck salt water and rocks at a depth of eighty feet, with the water in the hole rising to tide level. Therefore, the central boring was considered to have intersected the Flood Tunnel and charges of dynamite were set off in all holes, with the maximum charge of 160 pounds being packed into the centre hole. When detonation took place, observers at the Money Pit reported that the water in the pit began to boil and foam. Temporarily, at least, the water problem appeared to have been overcome.

The findings from the detonation drill-holes, Shaft No. 5, the Cave-In Shaft and the Money Pit itself suggest a certain profile to the Flood Tunnel (see Figure 16). This figure also includes the bedrock profile as defined by extensive drilling in recent years. Mining logistics virtually dictate the necessity to carry out the task of excavating a Flood Tunnel such as this from two ends. The complexity of the work at each end, the requirement to maintain uphill grades to facilitate the drainage of water from the working faces, ventilation requirements, removal of spoil, backfilling with beach stones and a host of other factors all had to be taken into account by those responsible for the execution of the work. The Flood Tunnel was a remarkable achievement, requiring skilled miners. The cunning nature of the inlet works is equally impressive. The complexity of this aspect of the Money Pit is considerably greater than that required to sink a shaft alone, and it would also have taken a considerably greater length of time. These considerations alone suggest that the two main elements of the project were carried out by different groups of excavators, with the Flood Tunnel and the inlet works at Smith's Cove post-dating that of the Money Pit.

Despite the complexity of the Flood Tunnel, the most important factor influencing construction was the general toughness of the glacial till through which the tunnel was driven. Only a nominal amount of timbering would have been required for support purposes, and only limited inflows of water would have been experienced.

Though the blasting at Smith's Cove was considered by the searchers to have been successful in rendering the Flood Tunnel ineffectual, water flowing into the Money Pit continued to hinder progress in excavating the shaft. The maximum pumping capacity that could be brought to bear only managed to maintain the water at the one hundred-foot depth: that is, eleven feet of water remained within the pit. William Chappell, a fellow director with Blair, decided to carry out some more borings within the Money Pit itself. Five borings were drilled from the surface with a working platform at the ninety-foot depth. Some intriguing evidence was recovered.

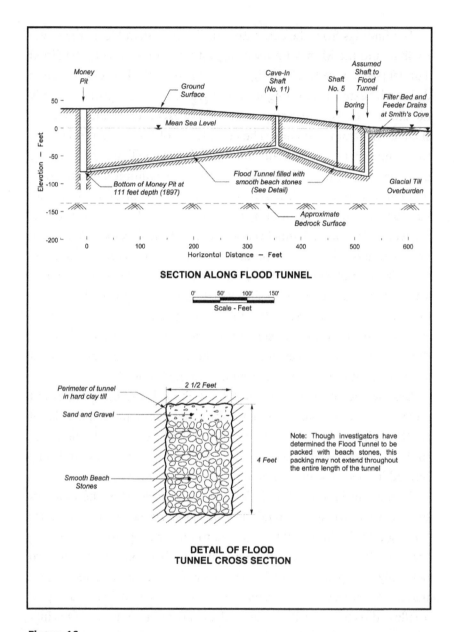

Figure 16

Section and Detail of Flood Tunnel from Money Pit to Smith's Cove as
Defined to 1897

The main purpose of the borings was to determine, if possible, the level to which the treasure chests had fallen during the 1861 collapse of the Money Pit. It is recalled that these supposed chests were supported on a platform of logs at the 105-foot depth. The holes were advanced by driving a three-inch diameter pipe with smaller pipes telescoped inside the larger pipe. No one expected to attain a depth greater than about 130 feet, as the greatest depth penetrated by adjacent shafts to that date had been 120 feet. In actual fact, the drillers penetrated to depths in excess of 170 feet due to the easy drilling conditions. The unexpected result of this work was exciting evidence of the inferred presence of metal bars and coin, located within a cement vault, between 153 and 160 feet below the surface. As a point of clarification the term 'cement' as used herein refers to some form of mortar, probably of water, lime and sand, and not to the modern cementitious material of the same name.

The results of the drilling program carried out in 1897 were recorded separately by Chappell and Blair, and the two accounts contain some differences in the recorded depths of the findings, but not in the materials encountered. Chappell's version of the drilling results was given in a sworn statement made in 1929. Blair's version is given by Harris in *The Oak Island Mystery* and by O'Connor in *The Big Dig*. The results of the five borings, including the two versions of the second boring in which cement and metal were reported at different depths, are summarized below. Figures 17 and 18 illustrate the findings of the second and third borings.

First hole:
- At 126 feet: 5 inches of oak wood and then iron.
- 126 feet to 132 feet: the 3-inch pipe could not be advanced past the iron at 126 feet, however a smaller drill was advanced to 132 feet.

Second hole from Chappell's statement (one foot away from the first):

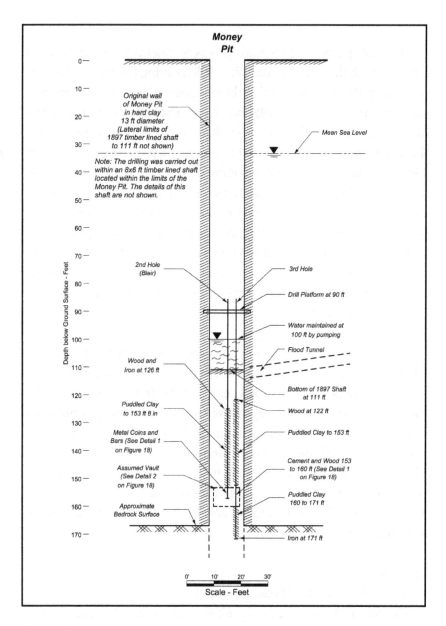

Figure 17

Results of Drilling in Money Pit by Oak Island Treasure Company in 1897

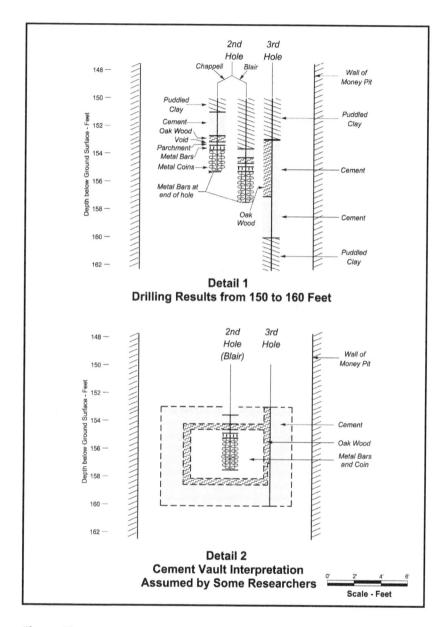

Figure 18

Details of Drilling in Money Pit by Oak Island Treasure Company in 1897

- At 126 feet: iron encountered and 3-inch diameter pipe could not be driven past the iron.
- 126 feet to 151 feet: 1½-inch diameter drill was able to bypass the iron obstruction and was advanced through puddled clay to 151 feet.
- 151 feet to 152 feet 8 inches: drilled through 20 inches of cement.

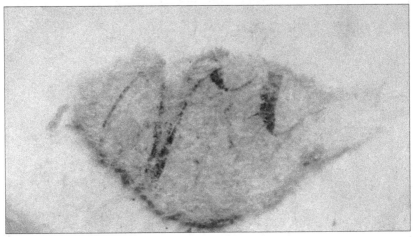

Photo 3 — Fragment of parchment recovered on auger in 1897 from a depth of 153 feet in Money Pit; fragment is 5/16 of an inch long.

- 152 feet 8 inches to 153 feet 1 inch: augered through 5 inches of oak wood.
- 153 feet 1 inch to 153 feet 3 inches: auger dropped 2 inches and came to rest on soft metal, fragment of parchment recovered from auger cuttings at this depth.
- 153 feet 3 inches to 155 feet 3 inches: used a boring chisel to advance through 4 inches of metal in bars and then 20 inches of coin or metal in small pieces.
- At 155 feet 3 inches: encountered metal in bars and boring chisel could not be advanced further

Second hole from Blair's record (one foot away from the first):

- At 126 feet: iron encountered and 3-inch diameter pipe could not be driven past the iron.
- 126 feet to 153 feet 8 inches: 1½-inch diameter drill was able to bypass the iron obstruction and was advanced through puddled clay to 153 feet 8 inches.
- 153 feet 8 inches to 154 feet 3 inches: drilled through 7 inches of cement.
- 154 feet 3 inches to 154 feet 8 inches: augered through 5 inches of oak wood.
- 154 feet 8 inches to 154 feet 10 inches: auger dropped 2 inches and came to rest on soft metal, fragment of parchment recovered from auger cuttings at this depth.
- 154 feet 10 inches to 157 feet 6 inches: used a boring chisel to advance through 4 inches of metal in bars and then 28 inches of coin or metal in small pieces.
- At 157 feet 6 inches: encountered metal in bars and boring chisel could not be advanced further.

Third hole:
- At 122 feet: 3-inch diameter pipe passed through wood.
- At 153 feet: 3-inch diameter pipe set solidly on cement.
- 153 feet to 157 feet: cement with oak wood on one side.
- 157 feet to 160 feet: cement.
- 160 feet to 171 feet: 11 feet of blue puddled clay.
- At 171 feet: solid iron obstruction.

Fourth hole:
- At 166 feet: struck iron obstruction but drill bypassed obstruction.
- At 188 feet: end of hole in hard clay.

Fifth hole:
- 150 feet to 170 feet: cement.
- At 175 feet: end of hole.

Chappell's statement contains some valuable observations, as illustrated by the following extracts.

He gave comments on the general soil types encountered:

> Most of the drilling was done in loose or soft, and what appeared to be disturbed ground, blue clay was encountered between 130 and 151 feet, and also between 160 and 171 feet. In one hole we appeared to be in a channel in which water was coming up... at the rate of 400 gallons per minute.

He observed:

> A ½ inch drill was put down past the obstruction and it went through blue clay to 151 feet and struck what appeared to be soft stone. Cuttings of this stone when compared, looked just like cement, and as analytical chemists subsequently pronounced samples from this material to have the composition of cement, it is hereafter referred to as cement.

He made conclusions regarding the twenty-four inches of material penetrated below 153 feet in the second hole:

> The conclusion was that the first four inches consisted of metal in bars which were pushed aside by the drill enough to permit it to pass, and that the additional twenty inches consisted of coin or metal in small pieces that fell into the space left by the tool as it was drawn up, and also that under these small pieces there was more metal (not iron) in bars.

He provided a description of the vertical contact between wood and cement below 153 feet in the third hole:

The three-inch pipe was then reset and another hole drilled, and the pipe put down until it rested solidly on the cement. At 153 feet we apparently touched wood on one side which extended down about four feet, the cement extending about three feet further to a depth of approximately 160 feet, with a total thickness of about seven feet from top of wood to bottom of cement.

He described in some detail the iron obstruction found in the third hole:

We then bored into a quite firm blue clay possessing the characteristics of puddled clay. This extended down to 171 feet where iron was struck. The iron was very solid, and the metallic sound could be plainly heard at the surface. We drilled on it two hours or more, getting into it not more than one quarter inch. The drill was taken out, sharpened and tempered for iron and two more hours in drilling and getting down another quarter inch.

Chappell's statement indicates that the soft stone encountered below 151 feet had the composition of cement, a conclusion based on analysis of samples reported to have the following average chemical composition:

Lime (CaO)	37.3%
Carbon Dioxide (CO_2)	33.8%
Silica (SiO_2)	13.6%
Iron and alumina	10.2%
Magnesium	5.0%
Moisture (at 120°C)	0.3%

Professional opinions given at the time of the discovery indicated the cement was the "work of man." This information, together with frenzied speculation concerning the nature of the metallic obstructions encountered in the drilling, were enough for the searchers to conclude that cement encased the treasure. This conclusion required a considerable extrapolation of the drilling results, as only a small part of the presumed cement vault with wood lining was actually defined by the drilling (see Figure 18).

The composition of the cement tabulated above can be evaluated in a general way. A pure limestone ($CaCO_3$) contains 44 per cent carbon dioxide (CO_2) and an impure limestone would contain less than this figure depending upon the amount of impurities, for example, iron, alumina, etc. Alternatively, a man-made cement of the period (probably consisting of a lime-based mortar) would be likely to contain a much smaller percentage of carbon dioxide, depending on the amount of sand incorporated into the mix and the extent of recarbonation. The cement could therefore have been an impure limestone, or dolomite, which contains a variable amount of magnesium, although the evidence is not conclusive. However, if the cement is not the work of man, and is in fact limestone, the question arises as to how the limestone came to be in the shaft at the levels reported. In this regard, it is known that the lower levels of the soil overburden do contain limestone boulders.

The recovery of a small scrap of parchment gave further heart to the treasure-seekers. It was about the size of a grain of rice in a rolled-up configuration and when unrolled proved to be oval-shaped and ⅜₆ of an inch long. It had what appeared to be the letters "v i" written on it in ink. Experts of the time identified the parchment as sheepskin with India ink lettering. The parchment is presently in the possession of Triton Alliance.

The exciting prospects of having shown that the Money Pit extended to at least 171 feet (how else could the iron plate struck at this level be explained?), and the smell of treasure in the form of coin and bar, prompted the directors to fund all further operations themselves. They immediately set about sinking Shaft No. 14 to a proposed depth of two hundred feet at a location forty-five feet south of the Money Pit (see Figure 15). Because the blasting at Smith's Cove had not fully cut off the water entering the Money Pit, it was concluded that there must be a second, lower Flood Tunnel. No thought seems to have been given to the possibility that this persistent inflow of water might be attributable to a natural water-bearing stratum at the base of the Money Pit or, as now considered more probable, solution channels within the underlying soluble bedrock induced by persistent pumping. The purpose of Shaft No. 14 was to locate such a lower Flood Tunnel and drain it, effectively emptying the upper levels of the Money Pit and enabling recovery of the presumed treasure vault between 153 and 160 feet.

Shaft No. 14 met the same fate as most previous shafts. No problems were encountered to a depth of ninety-five feet. However, water burst into the shaft some time later from an old tunnel that had been intercepted at seventy feet, and the ensuing rush of water drove the men from the shaft. This old tunnel was presumed to have been excavated by the Halifax Company in 1866--67. Undaunted, the company commenced Shaft No. 15 in 1898.

Shaft No. 15 (see Figure 15) was positioned thirty-five feet southwest of Shaft No. 14, and about eighty feet from the Money Pit. It is reported that though excavated through good, hard soil, the shaft encountered another old tunnel, this time at a depth of 105 feet. Once again this old tunnel was attributed to the activities of the Halifax Company. Throughout the records it has always been presumed that whenever old underground workings were encountered, for which there was no documentary evidence, the responsibility for these workings rests upon the Halifax Company, because of the secrecy with which they cloaked their activities. This may not be true. Such old workings, for which no provenance can be found, are more likely to originate from treasure recovery attempts immediately after the loss of the treasure, rather than by the Halifax Company.

Shaft No. 15 finally attained a depth of 160 feet, when salt water broke through into the bottom of the shaft via a seam of sand. This inflow of water could not be managed, excavation stopped and the shaft was abandoned. Later drilling at this location showed the bedrock to be at 170 feet.

In 1898 and 1899, a total of four more shafts was put down, with Shaft Nos. 16, 17, 18 and 19 being sunk to depths of 134 feet, 95 feet, 160 feet and 144 feet respectively (see Figure 15). All had to be abandoned because of water inflow, often accompanied by quicksand, similar to that encountered at Shaft No. 15. An interesting phenomenon was experienced, however, in Shaft No. 18, which was close to the Money Pit. After the 160-foot level had been attained and water began to rush into the shaft, the water in the Money Pit, initially at the seventy-foot level, fell fourteen feet as Shaft No. 18 began to fill with water, then rose back to its original level. This suggests a lower source of water feeding the Money Pit shaft. The quicksand conditions encountered at the bottom of these shafts suggest that the soils at depth, and closer to bedrock surface, are significantly more sandy than at higher levels, where the soils are predominantly clayey. In addition, the inability to reach bedrock surface in Shafts 15 to 19, which were not flooded out by adjacent tunnels, raises the question of how the original diggers were able to advance the Money Pit to such great depth without similar water and quicksand problems. This issue is discussed in Chapter 7.

The Oak Island Treasure Company resolved next to check on the effectiveness of the down-hole blasting used previously in an attempt to cut off the Flood Tunnel. A pump was located on the shore and water pumped into Shaft No. 18, which was known to communicate with the Money Pit. In expectation of muddy water emerging at Smith's Cove, they were surprised to find that muddy water emerged instead on South Shore at three entirely different locations. The precise locations are not recorded, but reference is made to their being at or beyond the low water mark. To confirm these startling results, they pumped water to which red dye had been added into the Money Pit, and dye-stained water emerged at the same three locations. To provide further corroboration, they exploded charges of dynamite on the South Shore (probably in the vicinity of where the dye-stained water had emerged) and commenced pumping from the Money Pit. Only a short time elapsed before muddy water was being extracted from the

Money Pit itself. The correct conclusion reached from this evidence was that a direct communication existed between the Money Pit and South Shore. The incorrect inference was that another man-made communication existed, feeding the Money Pit by means of a lower Flood Tunnel. Little, if any, credence was given to the possibility that this communication might be of natural origin. This was the case, as will be explained in Chapter 7 with reference to Figure 27. It is also significant that no evidence of a filter bed and feeder drains was found at the South Shore, nor has any such evidence been found to date. In any event, the absence of dye-stained water emerging at Smith's Cove indicated that the Flood Tunnel was at least partially blocked.

Further shaft-sinking began. Shaft No. 20 was put down immediately to the west of the Money Pit (see Figure 15), which partly overlapped the cribbing installed by the Truro Syndicate in 1850. Work proceeded apace, but at 113 feet depth water penetrated the shaft so rapidly that further excavation had to be abandoned. Because this shaft overlapped the west side of the Money Pit, excavation was partly in hard, virgin soil and partly in soft, infilled ground. It was observed that the core of soft clay within the Money Pit section appeared to be surrounded by an annulus of gravel, through which water flowed upwards. The soft clay infilling of the Money Pit could be removed easily without recourse to the use of a pick. Auger holes made to 126 feet, and believed to be within the Money Pit, disclosed only gravel, boulders and clay.

In 1900 the Oak Island Treasure Company attempted to raise more funds to finance further exploration work. The fundraising was a disappointment and Blair bought out the interests of the other directors, gaining full control of the company and its assets. By 1903 his funds were exhausted also, but he managed to obtain a long lease to the property, thereby gaining effective control over future work connected with the Money Pit and its elusive hoard. To date no evidence has been found of the presence of coin or metal in bars at the depth reported by Chappell and Blair.

CHAPTER 5

Important Evidence is Revealed

Glendower: I can call spirits from the vasty deep
Hotspur: Why, so can I: or so can any man:
But will they come, when you do call them?
"King Henry IV, Part I" (Shakespeare)

T he search for treasure on Oak Island had attracted the attention of a wealthy American engineer by the name of Captain Harry Bowdoin of New York. In 1909 he publicized his newly formed Old Gold Salvage and Wrecking Company and its intentions to resume the search for treasure on Oak Island. The company had an authorised capital of $250,000 and published its prospectus in great detail. Bowdoin had accepted the theory that the treasure was hidden by Captain Kidd, the notorious British pirate, and boasted "modern machinery and engineering science will solve in a jiffy the difficulties Captain Kidd made to guard his treasure." Though Bowdoin had never visited Oak Island and had no certain plans as to how to recover the elusive hoard, there was no uncertainty regarding his assessment of his own abilities to solve a problem that had consumed many other men's fortunes and careers.

The Old Gold Salvage and Wrecking Company commenced work in August 1909 with Bowdoin and his men setting up quarters on the island at his self-styled Camp Kidd. The first act was to clean out the old cross timbers and platforms in the Money Pit using a clam bucket. After this, an underwater inspection by a diver indicated an accumulation of planks and timbers oriented in all directions at the 107-foot depth. Further cleaning with the clam bucket was extended to 113 feet, and a program of drilling was carried out from the surface. The drill casing was set in the shaft, and drilling was started from a depth of 116 feet. The drill went through seventeen feet of gravel and sand, followed by sixteen feet of blue clay mixed with stones and sand. The drill then recovered a six-inch length of what appeared to be cement from a depth of 149 feet. Below 149 feet the drill then penetrated yellow clay and stones for a final eighteen feet before terminating on bedrock at 167 feet. Twenty-seven other borings, reaching bedrock between depths of 155 and 171 feet, showed similar results, including cement six to ten inches thick, but no positive, unequivocal evidence of either treasure chests or a treasure vault. There is some comment to the effect that a bright disc of metal was recovered in one length of core; regrettably, we know nothing else about it. The cement was submitted by Captain Bowdoin to Columbia University for analysis and reported to be "natural limestone pitted by the action of water." However, another report indicates the cement to be "rock-like material apparently man-made."

The drill findings suggest that the seventeen feet of gravel and sand encountered from 116 to 133 feet represents the annulus of washed gravel observed by the Oak Island Treasure Company at 118 feet in Shaft 20. It is of interest to highlight that Bowdoin did not encounter difficulties in penetrating wood and metal, as was the case for Chappell in 1897. It is likely, therefore, that Bowdoin's drilling was not centred within the Money Pit, but towards the side of the shaft. The depth to bedrock defined by Bowdoin is consistent with more recent drilling campaigns.

Blair, the holder of the lease, appears to have lost confidence in Bowdoin's abilities for some reason, perhaps due to Bowdoin's not having produced evidence of buried treasure. He refused to grant an extension of Bowdoin's permit. Bitterness arose and Bowdoin published an article in *Collier's Magazine* (August 11, 1911) with accusations that the treasure and Flood Tunnel did not exist. The substance of this debate is of little relevance to a meaningful interpretation of the facts surrounding the mystery of the Money Pit. The differences were not resolved and work on Oak Island thus ground to a halt in 1911 with Bowdoin's boastful assertions never having materialized.

Rudolphe Faribault visited Oak Island in 1911, and while compiling the first geological report of the region he concluded that limestone, gypsum, sandstone and shale were likely to occur below the thick overburden deposits at the east end of the island: this interpretation was subsequently proved correct. It was based upon an extension of the known bedrock geology from the mainland, where exposures are plentiful.

A number of adventurers appear to have been attracted to Oak Island between the years 1912 and 1931, however with little, if any, success. No major excavation work was carried out. Numerous theories and ideas were propounded, but when all is said and done, two decades were allowed to elapse with little factual knowledge gained that could help solve the mystery of the Money Pit and shed light on its originators. Only in 1931 did work recommence in earnest. In that year William Chappell, who had participated in Blair's first venture of 1894, returned to the scene.

The first order of business was to identify and stake out the location of the original Money Pit. There appears to have been some disagreement between Chappell and Blair as to its true location. The location for a new shaft was selected by Chappell and digging commenced. Blair was of the opinion that the location was six feet off. It appears that this new shaft, which later became known as the Chappell Shaft (Shaft No. 21), was located slightly southwest of the Money Pit (see Figure 19), and probably incorporated some of the earlier shaft work and cribbing. The shaft was reported to have plan dimensions of twelve feet by fourteen feet. As might be expected, excavation resulted in the disclosure of much of the earlier excavation cribbing. They managed to penetrate to a depth of 155 feet. This is considerably deeper than previous shaft sinking at the Money Pit and was achieved without major interruption by the inflow of water. Any water encountered appears to have been controllable by the pumping capacity immediately to hand. The artifacts encountered in this digging warrant special mention. They were:

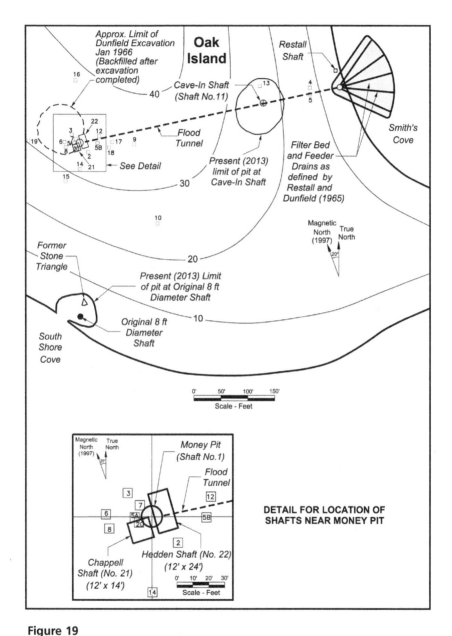

Figure 19

Location of Shafts and Pits Excavated to 1966

(1) An anchor fluke at a depth of 116 feet. The fluke was firmly embedded in the wall of the shaft. It was fouteen inches long, nine inches wide and 1¼ inches thick, and flatter than those of today. The rib of the fluke was on the inside of the curve. There was no sign of rust.

(2) A granite boulder at a depth of 119 feet. The boulder was about five feet in diameter and beneath it were fragments of wood, wood chips, spruce boughs and a limb of oak. The boulder required blasting to facilitate its removal.

(3) An axe at a depth of 123 feet. It was reported to be of obsolete pattern, the head being badly rusted but the wide blade clean. The wooden handle was straight and three feet long.

(4) A pick and the remains of a miner's oil lamp at 127 feet. The pick was small with one point oval, the other blunt and cross-hatched. The miner's lamp still contained oil, which was identified to be seal oil and, though the top was quite rusted away, the base was fairly rust-free.

(5) Various pieces of granite between 130 and 150 feet. The sizes are not reported but must have been fairly large to be worthy of mention, yet unlikely to approach those of the substantial boulder encountered at 119 feet.

The approximate locations where these objects were found are shown on Figure 20, which also shows results from excavation in the subsequent Hedden shaft to be discussed later. Unfortunately the anchor fluke, axe and pick, originally in the possession of Blair, have been lost, although photographs survive (see photos 4 to 8). It is noted that these photos were taken some years after recovery of the artifacts, since

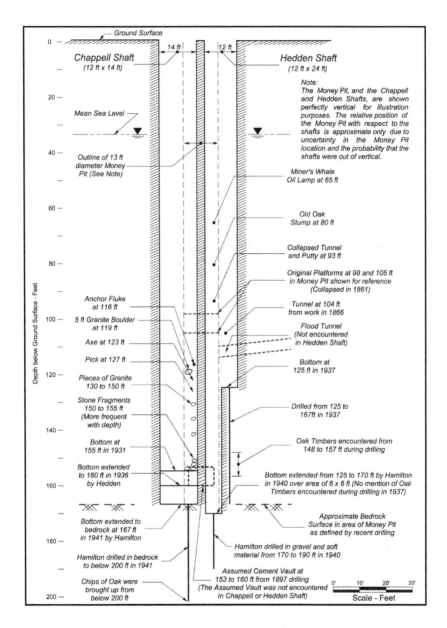

Figure 20

Section of Chappell and Hedden Shafts Excavated from 1931 to 1941

Photo 4 — Poll pick, felling axe and anchor fluke found in 1931 from 116 to 127 feet in Chappell Shaft.

Photo 5 — Felling axe found at 123 feet in Chappell Shaft.

Photo 6 — Close-up of felling axe.

Photo 7 — Poll pick found at 127 feet in Chappell Shaft.

Photo 8 — Close-up of poll pick.

Gilbert Hedden's brother-in law is in photos 5 and 7, and Gilbert Hedden did not appear on the scene until 1936. The artifacts are of considerable interest, as discussed below.

The anchor fluke, being of nautical origin, was probably brought to the workings from a vessel used by the original diggers, since searchers preceding Chappell were not able to excavate the Money Pit to the depth of 116 feet at which the anchor fluke was found. The anchor fluke was firmly embedded in the wall of the shaft, and the flat surface of the fluke could have been used as a shelf for an oil lamp. We have not researched the origin or type of anchor that would be consistent with the photo and dimensions of the fluke.

The axe is of great interest, and it is a pity it has since been lost. It was estimated at its finding to be of Acadian origin and 250 years old, though the basis for both these conclusions is unknown. This would imply that it dated from about 1680. Sally Ross and Alphonse Deveau, in their excellent book *The Acadians of Nova Scotia Past and Present*, state:

Written documents dating back to the 1680s and 1690s indicate that trade between the English in Boston and the Acadians in Port Royal was commonplace — despite the fact that it was officially illegal until the Treaty of Utrecht in 1713.

They state further that it was no secret "that the Acadians relied on the English, not the French, for salt and essential tools and utensils like harrows, ploughs, scythes, axes and knives."

The manifest of a ship laden at Boston and bound for Acadia on September 13, 1695, included an item of six-dozen axes. Thus it is difficult to reason why the axe recovered from the Money Pit was judged to be of Acadian origin.

Two of the key features of the axe are the long handle and the different types of metal used in the head and the blade. These features are described in various reports and are clearly illustrated in Photos 5 and 6. Henry Mercer, in his comprehensive book *Ancient Carpenters' Tools*, provides an excellent description of various axes in use in the

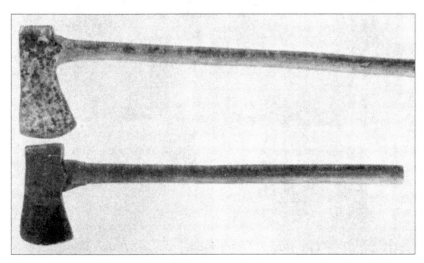

Photo 9 — Anglo-American felling axes dating to 1725 (top) and about 1750 (bottom).

eighteenth century, not only in America but also in the Old World. He provides many examples of American and Old World axes, and the type that best fits the axe found in the Chappell Shaft is identified as an "old Anglo-American felling axe" (see Photo 9), which evolved in the early 1700s with a combination of Old World and New World features. Mercer describes these axes as follows:

> The above described axes, whether of old European or American type, though used by carpenters, were more particularly the tools of the woodsman, and abundant evidence shows that until c.1840 they were generally home made, by local blacksmiths, of iron, with strips of steel inserted for the blade [see Photo 10], and the latter continued to make them, on special occasions, long after 1840, both in America and Europe.

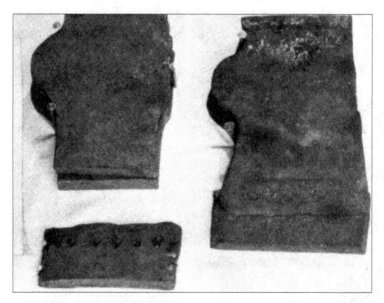

Photo 10 — Two stages of homemade axe, on left thin steel blade not yet placed and on right blade has received its first rough weld between two slabs of iron.

Considering the great length of time (over one hundred years), during which this type of axe head was made, and the diverse locations of its manufacture, it is not possible to accurately identify the date or origin of the axe found in the Chappell Shaft. However, it is clear that the normal use of such an axe would have been felling trees.

The pick found in the Chappell Shaft at a depth of 127 feet is referred to as a poll pick because of the one blunt end. We have reviewed historic reference material to determine what type of poll pick best fits the one found in the Chappell Shaft. Indeed, poll picks similar to that found were used in the sixteenth century, as recorded in *De Re Metallica* by Agricola. Considerable differences existed in the design of mining tools depending on the nature of ore, or rock, excavated. The appearance of this poll pick is identical to those favored by Cornish tin miners, and the following description is given in *Mining Tools* by William Morgan relating to poll picks used in Cornwall.

> One stem about 12 inch long from the end of the eye, and one stump about 3 inch long to form the poll. The eye is about 2½ inches long. When forged out of 1⅛ inches square iron — the thickest part of the stem — the head weighs about 4 lbs and is a favorite size for hard ground. The face of the poll is steeled like a sledge to form a pane [on which] to strike blows. 26 to 28 inches is a common length for the helve [handle].

This description is consistent with the poll pick from the Chappell Shaft. A sketch of the poll pick consistent with the above quoted dimensions is given in *Mining Tools*. This sketch is reproduced in the upper right corner of Photo 7 and the enlarged outline of the pick is superimposed on the photo of the pick in the hands of Hedden's brother-in law. There is convincing correspondence between the sketch and the actual picture of the pick recovered from the Money Pit.

The opinion recorded by Blair with respect to the axe, and the pick found four feet below, was that they belonged to earlier searchers and fell to their depths of 123 and 127 feet during the collapse of the Money Pit in 1861. Prior to the collapse of 1861, excavations in the Money Pit had extended to depths of ninety-three feet in 1804 and eighty-six feet in 1849. Therefore these tools would have had to drop some thirty to forty feet during the collapse to be consistent with Blair's theory. Also it was observed that both the axe and the pick were found in the vertical position and completely embedded in soft, disturbed or filled ground. This is not consistent with the random conditions that would be expected if the axe and pick were transported downward by the Money Pit collapse. Therefore, it is doubtful that the axe and the pick originated from the efforts of previous searchers. The conclusion must be reached that the axe and the pick encountered in the Chappell Shaft originate from work carried out prior to 1795.

The reports do not provide any information regarding the disposition of the various granite boulders encountered in the shaft. These may well have been located within the walls of the old Money Pit itself. The presence of a piece of oak beneath a boulder would suggest that the wood was being used as a lever in order to dislodge it, or as a wedge to prevent it from falling. A granite boulder of the largest size encountered in the Chappell Shaft would weigh between five thousand and six thousand pounds. Most likely the original diggers would have worked around such a boulder and left it in place.

It is also worth examining Blair's record with respect to conditions encountered deeper in the Chappell Shaft. He makes the observation that the soil in which they found themselves was much disturbed over half the shaft, and this is interpreted to mean half the plan area of the shaft being excavated. This observation is similar to that of the Oak Island Treasure Company during excavation of Shaft No. 20 some thirty years earlier. Blair's record mentions that at a depth of 150 feet within the disturbed half of the shaft they began to uncover fragments of stone that had the appearance of cement. Rupert Furneaux, in his well-known book, *Money Pit: The Mystery of Oak Island*, writes "that these discoveries perplexed Blair," and further that Blair reported the stone to have a "nature of which no person here can identify." Everyone engaged on the work must be assumed to have been familiar with local rock types, and those contained within the glacial till. One rock type, which does not outcrop, but which is now known to underlie the east end of the island, is gypsum/anhydrite, a relatively weak, water-soluble rock, not unlike cement in appearance and texture. Some basic chemical testing would have settled the issue. The stone fragments occurred occasionally at 150 feet, but became more numerous with increasing depth until they spread over the entire disturbed shaft area at 155 feet. These findings may be suggestive of a mine 'blow-out,' a violent and destructive event which could have resulted in a surge of invading debris from below. An alternative explanation is that the stone fragments are excavation debris brought to the surface while mining caverns at depth in the anhydrite/gypsum stratum and then used as backfill to the Money Pit shaft. This would imply that the stone fragments were placed by the original excavators of the Money Pit.

Chappell's work on Oak Island terminated in 1932. Some minor drilling was done in 1933 by John Talbot of New York, but with no noteworthy results. In the same year Blair made an agreement with Thomas Nixon of Victoria, British Columbia, and the Canadian Oak Island Treasure Company was formed with a capital of $225,000. Some drilling was done the following year (1934) with fourteen boreholes being put down to depths of up to 176 feet. The results were tantalising, with bits of oak and fragments of china being recovered from depth, the latter from below 123 feet. Shortly thereafter the company was disbanded.

It is uncertain as to when a driller named Baker put down some drill-holes in the vicinity of the Money Pit. The only reference to Baker's work is in *The Oak Island Enigma* by Leary, who records an exchange between Gilbert Hedden (the next searcher) and Baker in 1934. Therefore the drilling work by Baker was done prior to 1934 and may have formed part of the drilling performed by the Canadian Oak

Island Treasure Company, or it may have been a separate exercise. In any event it resulted in a finding of singular interest, although one that is not well documented. In one of Baker's drill-holes near the Money Pit he brought up specks of a silvery substance mixed up with the clay at the end of his boring tool. Inspection showed this substance to be free mercury.

Free mercury does not occur naturally, except in geologically unique circumstances. It is obtained by roasting cinnabar, or mercuric sulphide. It is used in gold separation and, prior to the middle of the nineteenth century, for producing tin amalgam as a backing to glass mirrors. Though Italy and Spain are presently the major producers of mercury, the United States and Mexico respectively rank third and fourth. The United States deposits are restricted to the states of California, New Mexico and Texas. In Mexico the mercury mines are west of Vera Cruz. Most of these New World sources were within the range of the Spanish conquistadors. Thus, a potential link exists between the contents of the Money Pit and New Spain.

In 1936 a dauntless adventurer, Gilbert Hedden from New York, assumed control of the Oak Island property. His first action was to set about cleaning and draining the Chappell Shaft (Shaft No. 21). His pumps were capable of handling one thousand gallons of water per minute, so he felt confident of his ability to handle water inflows. He reinstated the shaft to 150 feet, and from this depth he did some lateral probing with a drill-rig. Some bits of oak were the only findings of any interest. The shaft was extended to 160 feet with cribbing, the greatest depth yet attained at the Money Pit site, but nothing considered to be of any value was discovered.

The following year a new shaft was commenced, somewhat to the northeast (see Figure 19). This shaft was to be known as the Hedden Shaft (Shaft No. 22) and was fourteen feet wide by twenty-four feet long. Old shaft work was encountered almost immediately, the cribbing of which was apparently in good condition. Excavation ended at a depth of 125 feet, followed by borings to a further depth of forty-two feet, that is, to a total depth of 167 feet. The main findings from the shaft and the ancillary drilling are illustrated on Figure 20 and are listed as follows:

(1) At fifty feet old drill casings — at sixty-five feet an old miner's whale oil lamp — at eighty feet an old oak stump — at ninety-three feet an old collapsed tunnel with a band of putty in the vicinity.

(2) At 104 feet a tunnel was encountered measuring three feet ten inches wide by six feet four inches high cribbed with oak and hemlock timbers. (Blair was of the opinion this was part of a tunnel made about 1866 and certainly was not part of the original Money Pit construction.)

(3) Hard sand was encountered in the drill-holes between 125 feet and 148 feet, and oak timbers were penetrated in five borings between 148 and 157 feet, the timbers being of various thicknesses.

It is apparent that the Hedden Shaft did not intersect the Flood Tunnel, since no mention is made of it having been found. This suggests that the relative positions of the Hedden Shaft, the Money Pit and the Flood Tunnel as shown on Figure 19 are not correct, or that the end of the Flood Tunnel at the Money Pit was intersected but had been disturbed so much by previous searchers that it could not be identified. Hedden was not to do any more work on the island, but during his period there he is credited with making another mysterious find.

Hedden noted the considerable erosion of the shoreline at Smith's Cove. Close inspection revealed ancient-looking timbers projecting from the sand at low tide. Excavation of four feet of surface sand revealed these timbers to be gently inclined to the horizontal, about fifteen inches in diameter and four feet apart. Each horizontal timber was notched at four-foot intervals. Crosspieces pegged with wooden pins, or treenails, held the horizontals together. It was concluded that the structure was an old ramp or slipway.

Another discovery of Hedden's was a triangle of stones near the beach at South Shore Cove and two drilled rocks. Blair had also noted the stone triangle some forty years earlier but had not attached much significance to it. Hedden had found the stone triangle and drilled rocks using directions shown on a chart included in a book on Captain Kidd's treasure titled *Captain Kidd and His Skeleton Island*, written by Harold Wilkins and published in England in 1937. Hedden was struck by the similarity of descriptions on this chart to that of Oak Island. Despite this interesting coincidence, there is no direct connection between the island depicted on the chart and Oak Island. Other charts commonly referred to as the Kidd-Palmer charts also have been connected to Oak Island but the evidence is tenuous. More on Captain Kidd and interpretation of the charts can be found in *Treasure and Intrigue: The Legacy of Captain Kidd* by Graham Harris.

The stone triangle found by Hedden was located about forty feet from the beach and was about ten feet long on each side with a dividing line of rocks forming an 'arrow.' The drilled rocks were granite boulders with a uniform hole of 1½ inches diameter and 1½ inches depth on top of each boulder. Charles Roper, a surveyor from Halifax, was called in to survey the location of the stone triangle and drilled rocks, as well as other features of the site (see Figure 21). The survey showed that the central 'arrow' of the stone triangle pointed straight towards the Money Pit.

Hard on Hedden's heels came a very methodical adventurer by the name of Edwin Hamilton. Commencing the search in July 1938, he began by drilling fifty-eight lateral holes from various depths in the Hedden Shaft. He then commenced cleaning out the Chappell Shaft (Shaft No. 21) once again and retimbered it to 160 feet. During this excavation he came across an old Halifax Company tunnel which seemed to lead into the Money Pit at a location southeast of, and close to, Hedden's shaft. From this work he deduced that Chappell's shaft

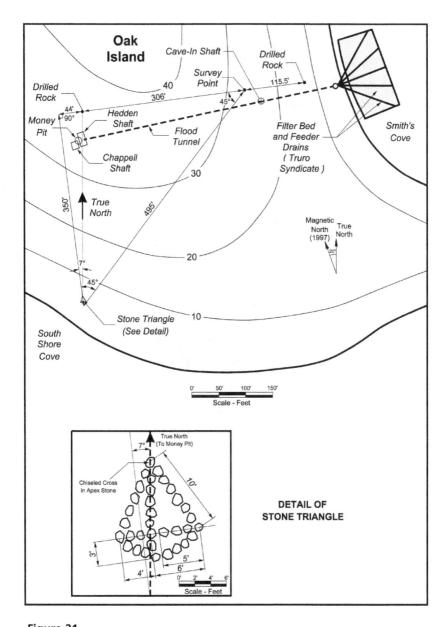

Figure 21

The Roper Survey of 1937

was about five feet from the actual Money Pit. In 1939–40 he extended the western part of the Hedden Shaft by sinking a shaft six feet square from a depth of 125 to 170 feet. Hamilton carried out some exploration drilling within his new shaft. One of the inconsistencies that he noted was the "presence of stones that were not native to that stratum of subsoil." These may have been fragments of rock from the underlying anhydrite bedrock.

Hamilton also deepened the Chappell Shaft from 160 to 167 feet, where bedrock was encountered. Drilling was carried out from the bottom of the Chappell Shaft to below two hundred feet, and in some holes chips of oak were brought up after penetrating a considerable thickness of bedrock. This astounding discovery is the first direct evidence of workings extending below bedrock surface. However, the

Photo 11 — Aerial view of Oak Island in 1938.

significance of these results may not have been realized at that time since efforts were obviously focused on recovering the treasure in the presumed vault at 153 to 160 feet depth. Some thirty years would pass before attention was directed to exploration of tunnels and caverns deep within the bedrock. From today's perspective, it is apparent that the bottom of the Chappell Shaft, which terminated on bedrock surface at a depth of 167 feet, was offset from the Money Pit Shaft, since the latter was subsequently proved as extending into bedrock. This is not consistent with Blair's report that the Chappell Shaft was partly within the disturbed backfill of the Money Pit. A possible explanation is that only the part of the Chappell Shaft within undisturbed original ground was extended to bedrock. Another possible explanation is that the original Money Pit may have had a 'dogleg' at the bedrock surface to follow a more readily excavated path through the bedrock, possibly even a natural soil-filled zone in the rock.

Hamilton is reported to have discovered a second, lower Flood Tunnel at a depth of 150 feet, approximately forty feet lower than the well-established Flood Tunnel that ran from Smith's Cove. It is claimed that this lower Flood Tunnel entered the Pit on its eastern side, the same side as the higher Flood Tunnel at 110 feet depth. Unfortunately the size, cribbing and packing of this lower tunnel are not given. In view of the lack of corroborative evidence, the existence of this second tunnel must be questioned.

Hamilton made some observations on the nature of water flow encountered in the Chappell Shaft. At a depth of 167 feet, the greatest depth anyone had yet penetrated, Hamilton observed "a flood of water eight by ten inches wide running from north-east to south-west across the site." This flow of water was clearly induced by the pumping operation that maintained the shaft dry. As such, the flow was not a natural underground stream but merely the flow of seepage water toward the dewatering sump. Samples of this water showed it to possess a higher specific gravity than sea water. No chemical analysis of this water seems to have been made. It would not be surprising, in view of the geology of the island, if the water contained a high percentage of calcium and sulphate ions.

Hamilton also carried out dye tests with rather interesting results. Dye introduced into the Chappell Shaft and Money Pit appeared unexpectedly in South Shore Cove about three hundred feet offshore from the high tide mark. The dye was observed from a boat to be discharging from the sea bottom at a point where the water depth was fifteen feet at low tide. It was assumed by the searchers that this was the inlet of a man-made Flood Tunnel to the South Shore, suggesting that the original workers had constructed a cofferdam to retain about twenty feet of water at high tide. This is extremely unlikely, even assuming that the mean sea level might have been several feet lower at the time of the original work. Hamilton's dye tests corroborated similar tests carried out four decades earlier by the Oak Island Treasure Company. Recent offshore surveys have found no trace of a cofferdam in this area. Hamilton suspended his operations in 1943 because of World War II.

CHAPTER 6

Tragedy and New Discoveries

For the Angel of Death spread his wings on the blast,
And breathed on the face of the foe as he passed
                    "The Destruction of Sennacherib" (Byron)

The period between World War II and 1955 was marred by ownership rights and other legal entanglements. Blair died in 1951 at the age of eighty-three, and the rights to the treasure trove on Oak Island eventually passed into the hands of Melbourne Chappell, a businessman from Sydney, Nova Scotia, and the son of William Chappell. Some token work was done by Chappell but this seems to have been minimal surface digging, the nature and extent of which are not in the public record. A Texas oil-drilling syndicate based in Corpus Christi then entered into an agreement and took up the reins. Led by George Greene, its work lasted a short four weeks during the summer of 1955.

Greene put down a line of boreholes on the north side of Shaft No. 21 (the Chappell Shaft) at varying distances between two and fourteen feet. The first borehole, closest to the shaft, struck various voids and attained a depth of 190 feet. The fourth, furthest removed, encountered oak timber eight inches thick at a depth of one hundred feet, a ten-foot void, eight inches of oak at 110 feet, a cavity from 110 to 155 feet, and then clay from 155 to 190 feet where the hole was terminated. By October 1955, Greene had returned to Texas, stating that they "poured 100,000 gallons of water into it [the cavity] and it [the water] ran out, but I don't know where."

William and Victor Harmon formed the next association with

Photo 12 — The Chappell Shaft in foreground and the Hedden Shaft at centre in 1955.

Melbourne Chappell to search for the elusive treasure. The Harmon brothers had considerable experience in exploration drilling for gold-mining ventures in Northern Ontario. They spent two months in the summer of 1958 drilling up to depths of 212 feet and brought up pieces of oak, spruce and coconut fibre from depths of more than 150 feet. Their work was terminated due to insufficient financing.

Two men, Robert Restall from Hamilton, Ontario, and Laverne Johnson from Vancouver, British Columbia, were next to arrive on the scene. They worked independently of each other, but the division of the rights ensured no conflict to their activities. Johnson does not appear to have carried out much excavation work. In 1962 he put down a series of drill-holes and made a small excavation to the north of the Money Pit. Apart from this limited amount of excavation work he appears to have spent a large amount of his time figuring out the 'whys and wherefores' of the Money Pit secret, making extensive use of the results of the Roper survey conducted in 1937. His musings, though of interest generally, are well documented elsewhere and do not concern us in this volume.

Restall and his family lived and worked on the island for five years. Being a family operation and working without heavy equipment, their progress was inevitably slow. A considerable effort was spent exploring the remnants of the filter bed system in an attempt to identify the key to stopping the flow of water from Smith's Cove. Restall found extensive evidence of the filter bed in the form of eel grass, coconut fibre and sections of the feeder drains. However, he was not able to find the point at which the feeder drains entered the vertical shaft to the Flood Tunnel. He then attempted to locate the Flood Tunnel by excavating shafts near the shoreline at Smith's Cove.

It was a hot, close August day in 1965 when Robert Restall, his son (also named Robert) and helpers Cyril Hiltz and Carl Graeser were killed in one of the shafts they had dug close to Smith's Cove. They were running a pump to remove water from a shaft they had excavated. It is reported that Restall, while leaning over the top of the twenty-seven-foot deep shaft to check the water level, was overcome by carbon monoxide fumes from the pump and fell. His son went down the shaft to rescue him, and others followed. In the end four were dead and four rescuers had to be treated. The known tally of dead among the treasure-seekers on Oak Island had now reached six, a man having been scalded to death in 1861 when a boiler burst and a man having fallen to his death in a shaft in 1897 after a hoist-rope broke.

During his period on the island, Restall is credited with having discovered a stone inscribed with the date 1704. This dating led Restall to believe that the treasure had been buried in that year. However, it could also indicate a time when people were on the island trying to recover the treasure.

In 1965 Robert Dunfield, a geologist from California, took up the search with considerable eagerness. He had visited the island during Restall's tenure, and was excited to try his hand where many had failed before. He appears to have inspired twenty-four others to fund his syndicate. One of the tasks completed by Dunfield was the preparation of detailed sketches of the Money Pit and Smith's Cove filter drain areas in July 1965. His sketch of the filter drain system incorporates the results of extensive explorations by Restall. The Dunfield sketch is reasonably consistent with the descriptions by Adams A. Tupper, based on the first exposure of the filter system in 1850. The main difference between the two versions is that the shape of the deep zone filled with beach stones is rectangular in Tupper's description but triangular in Dunfield's sketch. The filter drain configuration developed by Dunfield is illustrated later on Figure 24, along with further discussion on this matter.

The main thrust of Dunfield's operation was to utilise heavy earth-moving equipment on a scale that had not been seen before. The first thing he did was to construct a causeway to the island to facilitate the movement of equipment, men and materials to the site. Before the construction of this causeway the only access had been by boat. He estimated, before he commenced serious digging, that the work could be completed in about three weeks. He was, however, prudent enough to add that actual progress depended on the discoveries they would make on a day-by-day basis.

Excavation started in October 1965 with the digging of a trench along South Shore to intercept and block the presumed second flood tunnel. The trench was excavated to a depth of twenty feet over a length of two hundred feet, and no second flood tunnel was encountered. However, in one part of the trench, an eight-foot diameter backfilled shaft was found about twenty-five feet south of the stone triangle (see Figure 19). The distinct circular shape of the shaft was clearly evident at a depth of twelve feet below surface, and pick marks were observed on the side walls. Based on the absence of cribbing in the shaft, and since no previous digging had been done in this area, the shaft was attributed to the original depositors. The excavation was deepened to explore its extent and was terminated at fifty-four feet, which was thought at that time to be the bottom of the shaft. It suggested that the shaft had been abandoned without a connection being made to any other underground workings. It is now thought this shaft may have been excavated as part of an attempt to begin a flood tunnel linking the Money Pit to South Shore, a much shorter distance than to Smith's Cove. The circumstances suggest the attempt failed, and these are discussed in Chapter 11.

On November 3, 1965, the excavation equipment was moved to the Money Pit, where Dunfield started digging a 'glory hole,' which would eventually become some eighty to one hundred feet wide at the top and 135 feet deep. During the early part of the excavation, Dunfield recorded an interesting observation regarding the location of the original Money Pit in his report dated November 4, 1965:

> At 8:00 a.m., November 4, 1965, we reached a depth of 22 feet and we have observed ½ to ⅔ of the original money pit well defined immediately north of the Chappell Shaft.

Excavation continued in November to a depth of 132 feet, at which time there was a delay of three weeks to mobilise a bigger dragline. During the delay some sloughing of the excavation slopes and shifting of the old shafts occurred. Digging resumed on December 24, 1965 (with shutdown for December 25 and 26), and a depth of 135 feet was achieved. Rain caused problems in the form of slope failures and shaft deformation. Dunfield's report dated January 6, 1966, states:

> On January 1, 1966, the Chappell shaft partially collapsed
> along with complete collapsing of the 1804 and 1863 shafts
> to the southwest. The enormous hole was now 80' in diam-
> eter and the Hedden shaft began shifting to the west. On
> January 2, 1966, it was necessary to make a decision to fill
> the hole using both the crane and the dozers for the pur-
> pose of saving the Hedden shaft and the submersible pump.
> Filling the hole took three, 10 hour shifts, and the Hedden
> shaft had been saved although it had buckled and moved
> west about 4'.

*Photo 13 — Dragline excavation by Dunfield at Money Pit in January
1966; top part of Chappell shaft at right has collapsed and northwest
corner of Hedden shaft at left is intact. (Video image)*

The backfilled excavation was graded to a level about eleven feet below original ground surface to permit drilling in the vicinity of the Money Pit. In addition to this 'glory hole,' Dunfield also excavated a huge crater 108 feet deep at the location of the Cave-In Shaft, but without locating the Flood Tunnel.

Although remnants of the Hedden Shaft can be seen to this day, Dunfield's work on Oak Island was massive and destructive. Unfortunately, there was little sensitivity in his approach that would have allowed recovery of vital evidence and clues, although it is understood that some coarse screening and washing of the excavated spoil was carried out. The scars of Dunfield's work still remain as a depressed area at the Money Pit, an open pit on the South Shore and an open pit at the Cave-In Shaft.

While on the site, Dunfield carried out more exploratory drilling at the Money Pit to depths of up to 190 feet. Apparently he found the same cavity penetrated by Greene in 1955. At a depth of 140 feet (just below the terminal depth of his excavation) the drill encountered a two-foot layer of limestone and then fell through forty feet before terminating on rock at 182 feet. Samples of the rock are reported to have looked like cement, but after being sent away for analysis were confirmed to be gypsum. Dunfield finished his work on Oak Island in April 1966 and returned to California. According to the *Chronicle-Herald* of March 15, 1966, Dunfield is claimed to have disclosed the presence of an underground chamber located between 139 and 184 feet below ground. It was described as being roofed with wood and floored with iron.

Evidence of large cavities found in close proximity to the Money Pit was reported by Thomas Nixon (1934), George Greene (1955) and Dunfield (1966). The depths at which these cavities were reported are not within a consistent range. Some doubt must exist, therefore, as to whether these reported cavities were indeed open 'chambers' as has been intimated, or whether the falling of the drill rods through very soft soil had suggested their presence.

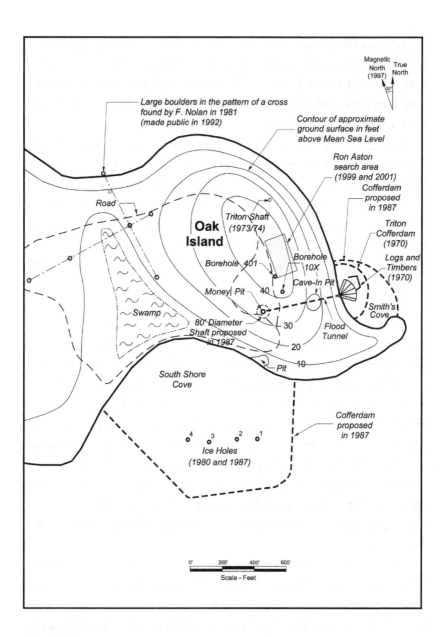

Figure 22
Location of Oak Island Activities from 1966 to 2005

From 1966 to 2005, the exploration work on Oak Island has been driven by the team of David Tobias, a businessman from Montreal, and Dan Blankenship, a contractor from Florida. Their efforts, spanning a period of some forty years, have revealed greater depths of original workings at the Money Pit than had ever been imagined during the previous 170 years of searching. Figure 22 shows the location of some of the key activities on Oak Island from 1966 to 2005.

In 1966 Blankenship excavated to a depth of ninety feet at the shaft that Dunfield found near the stone triangle. The shaft did not terminate at fifty-four feet as had been previously assumed. At sixty feet Blankenship found a hand-wrought nail. From a depth of sixty-five to seventy-seven feet he found distinct alternating layers of red sandy soil and blue clay, which he referred to as man-made puddled clay. This was underlain by eight feet of black muck and a five-foot layer of rounded granite boulders in "a pool of black stagnant water." The excavation could not be deepened due to caving ground. The remnants of this digging can be seen to this day as a water-filled pit adjacent to the shoreline. Blankenship's discoveries are significant as they confirm the likelihood of an earlier attempt to excavate a flood tunnel from South Shore.

In 1967 a program of about forty-five deep holes in bedrock was carried out in the area of the Money Pit using a Becker type drill. The results of this drilling program were to provide the sensational information that would spur the interest of searchers for the next thirty-five years. David Tobias wanted to drill deeper than the maximum depth of 167 feet below original ground level reached by previous excavators, to ensure that any man-made workings found below this depth could be argued to be original work. Tobias was not aware of the oak chips found in the bedrock (at more than two hundred feet depth) during the 1941 drilling by Edwin Hamilton, and this was not the factor leading to the deep-drilling program. The underground picture that evolved from the drilling is illustrated on Figure 23, which is a cross-section through the Money Pit. For continuity with previous explorations, the depth

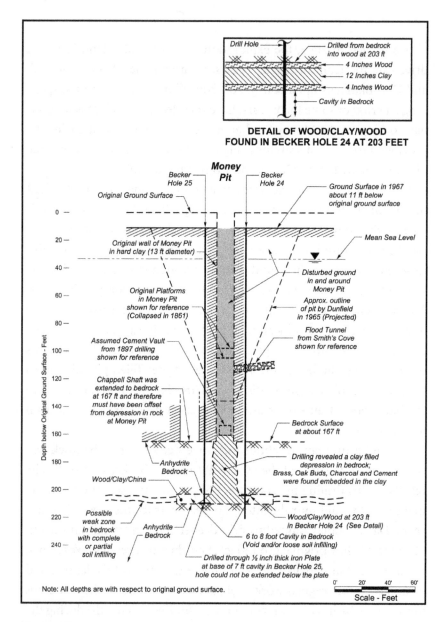

Figure 23

Results of Drilling In and Around Money Pit by Triton Alliance in 1967

Photo 14 — Exploration in winter of 1967 with Becker drill, Hedden Shaft to right of drill.

Photo 15 — Piece of brass recovered in 1967 from 187 feet below original ground (or higher) in Becker drill-hole 21 at Money Pit.

reference in the Becker holes is with respect to the original ground surface, which was eleven feet higher than at the time of drilling.

One of the fascinating features to emerge from evaluation of the numerous drill-holes was the presence of a soil-filled depression extending about forty feet below the surrounding bedrock surface. Though not accurately defined, the depression was roughly circular with a diameter somewhat larger than that of the Money Pit. The soil infilling was described as a grey or blue puddled clay and was assumed by Tobias and Blankenship to represent fill used to seal the Money Pit. A fragment of brass was recovered in Becker hole 21 from a depth of 187 feet (or at some higher location) below the original ground surface, which is equivalent to a depth of 176 feet below the ground surface at the time of drilling. Based on the high concentration of impurities found from an analysis of the brass, it was estimated by experts to have been manufactured prior to the middle of the nineteenth century.

The holes close to the Money Pit suggested a highly irregular bedrock surface below which were encountered natural cavities partially filled with soft soil, or man-made chambers, 6 to 8 feet high at several locations. In Becker hole 24, where a bedrock cavity was encountered from 203 to 210 feet, the findings were of singular interest. In this hole a sequence of wood/clay/wood was encountered directly below the roof of the cavity (see detail on Figure 23). The recovered wood (from 203 feet) was later carbon dated at AD 1575 ± 85 years, giving an implied time span between 1490 and 1660. In Becker hole 25 a seven-foot cavity was found from 202 to 209 feet and then a ½-inch thick iron plate was penetrated with the diamond drill. Although the cored disc from the iron plate was not recovered, the identification of iron was based on the unmistakable sound of a diamond drill bit cutting through a solid metal object. However, the hole could not be advanced below the iron plate, and thus it was not possible to determine if it was the cover of an iron-lined treasure vault. Pieces of china, cement and more wood were also recovered from the cavity. Becker hole 35, located on the edge of the clay-filled depression, proved bedrock between 171 and 189 feet, then wood to 191 feet. The following twelve feet, to a final depth of 203 feet, penetrated a void (either natural cavity or chamber) from which were recovered fragments of wood, charcoal and clinker. These findings imply the existence of a close arrangement of cavities (or chambers) within the bedrock that contain incontrovertible evidence of past human activity.

Of particular interest are the results of the carbon-14 dating from the sample of wood recovered from Becker hole 24, though the dating range inferred from the testing may not be as accurate as it might seem. All living organisms absorb carbon-14 from the environment. When an organism dies, the radiation 'count' decreases as a result of the radiation decay process. Thus, a tree that has grown for one hundred years before being felled and subjected to carbon-14 dating immediately after felling will show an age of one hundred years in the centre heartwood, whereas the age of the outermost sapwood will be

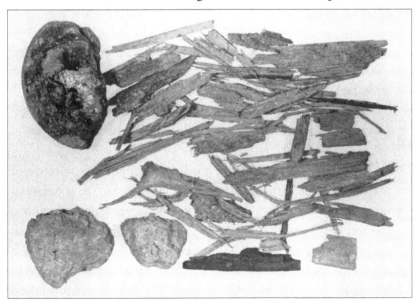

Photo 16 — Pieces of wood and red brick-like material brought up in 1967 from a bedrock cavity at 203 feet below original ground in Becker drill-hole 24.

theoretically only several years. Since there is no knowledge of the exact part of the tree from which the test sample originated, the dating may be in considerable error. The date of 1575 should be considered the earliest possible date that the tree was felled. If the sample originated from within the tree's heartwood, the actual date of felling could be considerably later, possibly by one hundred years or more. The experimental or statistical error implicit in this type of test (±85 years) may be small in comparison to the variation that results from the position of the wood sample within the tree, or what is sometimes referred to as the 'old wood effect.'

The results of the 1967 drilling program provided convincing evidence of man-made underground workings in the bedrock at depths of more than two hundred feet below the original ground surface. These findings resulted in the formation of Triton Alliance Ltd. in April 1969 with the influx of new working capital. David Tobias, who headed up the group, sponsored the 1967 drilling program and stated:

> It [the drilling] located wide areas of bedrock 165 feet down and a peculiar depression where the bedrock was not reached until 200 feet plus. The drill went through the 165 feet levels of bedrock around this depression. Four cavities were found beneath the bedrock, at levels deeper than 200 feet.

The discoveries at the Money Pit quickly changed the objective of the search from the assumed vault at 153 to 160 feet, to a potential treasure cavern deep within the bedrock. Additional drilling programs (to 250 feet depth) were carried out for Triton Alliance by Warnock Hersey in 1969 and by Golder Associates in 1970, to define subsurface conditions for the design and construction of a deep excavation and to further explore the caverns in the bedrock. The drilling extended deep into the rock and defined an extensive system of natural and possibly man-made caverns in the bedrock, some of which were partially or completely soil filled. The caverns extended for distances of up to several hundred feet from the Money Pit and were typically five to ten feet in height with some twenty to forty feet of bedrock cover. Investigation of these caverns was to preoccupy Triton for some time.

The drilling carried out by Golder Associates produced excellent intact samples of soil infilling material in the rock cavities, and selected samples were submitted to Dalhousie University for palynological (pollen type and frequency) analysis in an attempt to identify their age. Two samples recovered in the depth range of 215 to 218 feet at Borehole 102, located 50 feet south of the Money Pit, showed characteristics of ancient glacial till, with no evidence of more recent soil being present. Two samples of soil infilling recovered from a depth range of 193 to 198 feet in Borehole 103, located at the Money Pit, were at considerable variance with those in Borehole 102, as described in the report by Professor J.C. Ritchie of Dalhousie University:

Photo 17 — Aerial view of Oak Island in 1970 showing cofferdam and excavation at Smith's Cove; Money Pit is at white arrow.

Photo 18 — Aerial view of excavation at Smith's Cove in 1970 showing part of U-shaped log structure.

Photo 19 — Close up of U-shaped log structure exposed in 1970 excavation.

Photo 20 — Remnant of inclined timber connected to horizontal log in 1970 excavation.

Photo 21 — Horizontal timbers and remnants of inclined timbers connected to log in 1970 excavation.

The occurrence of aggregations of typical post-glacial and recent pollen types in addition to the 'normal' rare isolated pollen types (*Carpinus, Ulmus*) suggests strongly that recent or post-glacial material has been mixed secondarily with the primary matrix. In other words, the palynological evidence suggests that the original material has been disturbed, causing a palynological anomaly.

The samples from Borehole 103 were clearly shown to include recent surface soils, thus providing verification of man-made soil infilling at great depth in the Money Pit as concluded from the drilling results.

In the summer of 1970, Triton constructed an earth cofferdam to isolate the filter bed at Smith's Cove for further exploration. The new cofferdam was further offshore than previous cofferdams constructed by the Truro Syndicate in 1850 and the Halifax Company in 1866. It extended beyond the low tide level but was not strong enough to withstand severe storm events. Eventually it was overtopped, but not before Triton made several interesting discoveries. Digging within the cofferdam exposed, among other things, the remnants of an elaborate timber structure that became the subject of much conjecture and study.

The timber structure was found below several feet of sand. The most striking feature of the old timber structure was a U-shaped configuration of logs to which horizontal and inclined timbers were attached at regular intervals (see photos 17 to 21). The inclined timbers were hewed to a rectangular shape and were attached to horizontal circular logs by wooden dowels in the same fashion as those exposed by Hedden in 1937. Only a small length of the inclined timbers remained attached to the logs, and beside each inclined timber the logs were typically marked with sequential Roman numerals. Some sections of the inclined timbers had sawn boards attached in a horizontal configuration. The location and elevation of the log structure was carefully surveyed by Triton, together with other features of the excavation, including a log ramp found below the old wharf. However, Triton was not able to accurately define the location of the original filter bed system and the five radial drains before the cofferdam was overtopped.

A common assumption by most searchers was that the log structure was part of the cofferdam works used to construct the original filter bed and feeder drain system. In order to evaluate this assumption, we examined the position of the log structure with respect to available information on the layout of the original filter system. We found that there were sufficient reference points to superimpose the drain layout defined in Dunfield's sketch of July 1965 (see earlier discussion) on the surveyed location of the log structure. The resulting correlation is illustrated on Figure 24. It is clearly evident that the log structure does not enclose the entire drain system. This was verified based on personal communication with Dan Blankenship. He observed parts of the original drains to the south of the log structure during the 1970 excavation. However, based only on geometrical considerations, there are two possible scenarios that are consistent with the log structure being part of the original filter drain construction.

The first scenario would involve the exposed log structure representing only part of the cofferdam, with the other part either still in place or removed by the original constructors. Since both ends of the log structure were exposed, this scenario is more consistent with removal of part of the cofferdam by the original workers, possibly for recovery of the timber. In the second scenario, the log structure would have served some other purpose for the original workers, although we have not speculated on such possible use.

An alternative explanation for the presence of the log structure is that it was part of the work done by the Halifax Company in 1866. The prospectus of the Halifax Company called for construction of a cofferdam using wood and clay. The length of the exposed log structure is about 155 feet, which is considerably less than the cofferdam length of 375 feet reported by Adams A. Tupper. However, if the two end sections of the log structure were extended just beyond the high water mark by earth fill, the total cofferdam length is then in very close

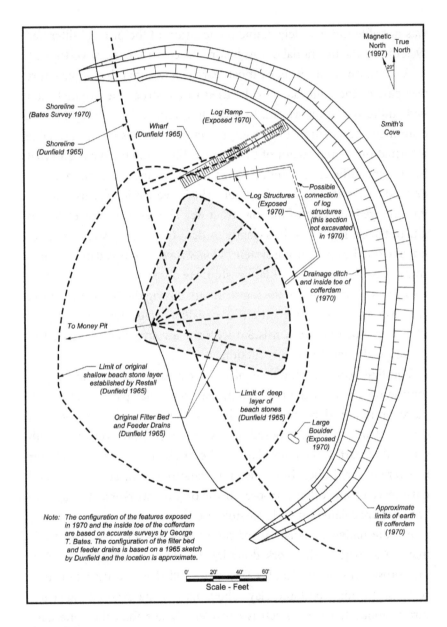

Figure 24

Plan of 1970 Excavation at Smith's Cove Showing Log Structure and Original Filter Bed and Feeder Drains

agreement with the value of 375 feet. Also, the section of the log structure furthest from the shore was about nine feet below current high water level at large (spring) tide (about Geodetic elevation minus 5½ feet), which is consistent with the cofferdam height of twelve feet reported by Tupper. The practice of chiseling Roman numerals upon precut timbers, to denote the sequence in which they were to be incorporated into construction, is an ancient practice. Numerous examples have been discovered during demolition of old building in Halifax alone.

The timber ramp-type structure to the north of the log structure was at a somewhat higher elevation and thus may or may not be of the same period as the log structure. It is possible that the timber ramp was used as a slipway, or dock, for the berthing of vessels unloading materials and supplies. If of the same period, the non-parallel orientation of the ramp and the north leg of the log structure is consistent with the presence of clay fill, of increasing width with increasing water depth, separating the ramp and the north leg.

As will be shown later in this chapter, there is an immense discrepancy in the results of carbon dating on samples of wood and coconut fibre recovered from the original construction. Overall the results extended over several centuries, clearly a time span of little utility. However, for demonstration purposes, if it is assumed that the filter system was constructed in 1300, sea level would have been about seven feet lower than it is at present, but the tidal range would have been the same. The range of large tides at Mahone Bay is about seven feet and, since such tides occur twice per month, this is the tidal range that would have to be managed during construction, in addition to wave and storm surge effects. The high-tide line in 1300 would be roughly equivalent to the present low-tide line. For the Flood Tunnel system to work, a filter system would logically have been constructed between the high-tide and low-tide lines, with a temporary cofferdam located at or close to low-tide level. Therefore, the position of a filter drain system constructed in 1300 would be located offshore of the present low tide line, which is not the case. If this line of reasoning is applied to the location of the filter system exposed at Smith's Cove, its construction would likely have been after about 1700. This date does not necessarily apply to the Money Pit, which could have been dug earlier.

The excavation at Smith's Cove exposed a number of interesting artifacts, some of which were recovered from several feet below the level of the log structure. Some of these artifacts could be associated with the original construction of the filter drain system. The artifacts include a heart-shaped stone; a pair of ancient wrought iron scissors reportedly found below one of the original drains; a small wooden sled (or skip) found about three feet below the log structure; a twelve-inch long segment of a wrought iron ruler (or part of a set square) found beside a notched log and various iron nails, spikes and tools.

The heart-shaped stone was examined by the Smithsonian Institution and was reported to be "a man-made shape." The scissors were also examined by the Smithsonian Institution and identified as typical Spanish-American design that were "made in this manner as late as the mid-19th century in North Mexico and Southwest United States." The sled was eighteen inches wide by twenty-four inches long and could have been used in removing tunnel spoil from the Smith's Cove section of the Flood Tunnel. The ruler was examined and analysed by Allan B. Dove, of The Steel Company of Canada. He indicated in his report dated December 14, 1970, that it was made of wrought iron and that the markings were hand-engraved. He could not determine an accurate age for the ruler but as a guess placed the date before 1783, based on microscopic examination of the wrought iron matrix. The nails, spikes and tools were also studied by Dove, and in his report dated September 25, 1970, he described the specimens as hand-forged wrought iron dating prior to 1790, with one exception. That exception was determined as being machine-sheared from wrought iron plate about $\frac{5}{32}$ inches thick. Henry Mercer in *Ancient Carpenters' Tools* refers to these as cut nails and indicates that this type of nail was produced in America from 1800. This suggests that the two types of nails come from two separate periods of activity.

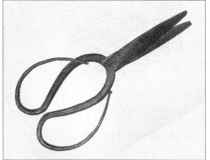

Photo 22 — Heart shaped stone found in 1970 excavation at Smith's Cove.

Photo 23 — Spanish-American scissors found in 1970 excavation at Smith's Cove.

Photo 24 — Wood box found 3 feet below U-shaped log structure in 1970 excavation at Smith's Cove.

Photo 25 — Wrought iron ruler with hand engraved markings found in 1970 excavation at Smith's Cove.

Carbon dating of various wood samples from the log structures and other wood artifacts from the cofferdam excavation was carried out, and the results give ages ranging from about one hundred to four hundred years before present (1950), covering the period of about 1550 to 1850. The 'old wood effect' discussed earlier could place the felling of the trees some one hundred or more years later in time, however, and a plus or minus range of some thirty to one hundred years applies to the test results. It is clear that the carbon dating results are not of much value in resolving the date of the Smith's Cove works.

Carbon dating was also carried out in 1990 on two coconut fibre samples. The first sample was recovered from Smith's Cove by Dan Henskee in 1990 after removal of several feet of sand and gravel. The second was an existing sample obtained from David Tobias. The samples were sent by Triton to the laboratory of Beta Analytic Inc. in Florida, and the results gave respective ages before present (1950) of 770 ± 60 years and 820 ± 70 years, corresponding to dates of AD 1180 ± 60 years and AD 1130 ± 70 years.

In 1996, as part of a study carried out by the Woods Hole Oceanographic Institute in Maine, two additional coconut fibre samples were carbon dated. The first sample was recovered from Smith's Cove in 1996 by Dan Henskee in the presence of Woods Hole personnel, and the second was an existing sample in storage. The samples were sent to the National Ocean Sciences AMS Facility, a part of the Oceanographic Institute, for carbon dating. AMS refers to Acceleration Mass Spectrometry, a test method that requires only small samples. The tests gave respective ages before present (1950) of 1140 ±30 years and 765 ± 35 years, corresponding to dates of AD 810 ±30 years and AD 1185 ± 35 years. We have no reasonable explanation for these results, but it is well known that massive effusions of 'dead' carbon dioxide (which contains no carbon-14) are discharged during volcanic eruptions. These affect the accuracy of radio-decay dating techniques. Also the earlier discussion, regarding the effect of a lower sea level on the position of the filter drain system, excludes these carbon dates as being representative of the original Smith's Cove construction.

We can now summarize the survey data, metal analysis and carbon dating results as they relate to an interpretation of the sequence and date of the works exposed in the cofferdam at Smith's Cove. The survey information (Figure 24) indicates that the U-shaped log structure does not entirely enclose the feeder drains. However, it could have been constructed at the same time as the drains, and the most likely scenario in this case would have been partial removal of timbers by the original workers. The preponderance of present evidence suggests that most of the work at Smith's Cove was executed in the period of about 1700 to 1800 and that the U-shaped log structure itself was part of the original work or was part of the searchers' work in 1866. Further investigation by excavation within a cofferdam, with appropriate archaeological analysis, would be expected to better define the construction sequence and age of the flood system at Smith's Cove.

Another interesting feature was discovered near the shoreline within the cofferdam at Smith's Cove, where it was reported:

> The earth towards the shore showed evidence of extensive heat and was burnt deep red with patches of white in layers. Pieces of charcoal and coal were found.

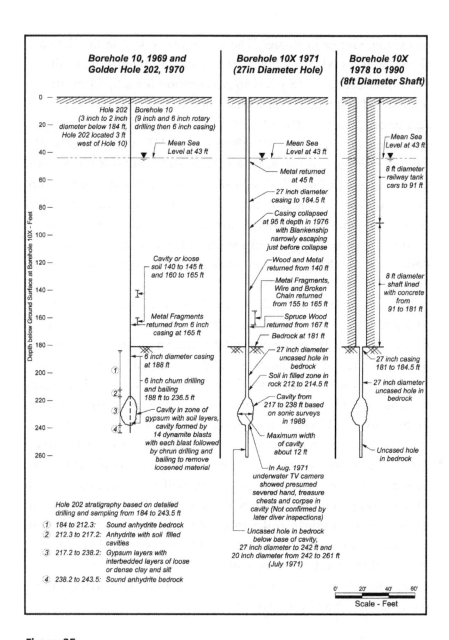

Figure 25

Main Findings in Borehole 10X from 1970 to 1990

This is likely to have been the site on which a furnace was operated to provide ventilation air for that section of the Flood Tunnel being commenced from the Smith's Cove end (reference may be made to Figure 7). The chimney to the furnace would have been masked from the ocean by the tall oaks growing on the point of land known as Isaac's Point (see Figure 3). In fact this point would have screened all operations in Smith's Cove from the open sea.

In 1969 Dan Blankenship was dowsing in an area northeast of the Money Pit and reported in later correspondence that, "I would dowse in an effort to locate what I would consider the most promising of these areas, eventually deciding upon the location where hole #10 was placed." This location, 180 feet northeast of the Money Pit, was to become the site of extensive drilling, blasting, shaft sinking and speculative findings for the next twenty-five years. Dowsing is a non-scientific method of locating underground features, and is more commonly associated with the ancient art of finding underground aquifers suitable for development of water wells. A lighthearted assessment of dowsing was reported in the journal *Ground Engineering*, based on experiments by John Greenwood at a seminar held at Nottingham Trent University in June 2000.

The key findings in Borehole 10, Borehole 10X (at the same location as Borehole 10), and Shaft 10X are discussed below and are illustrated in Figure 25. Borehole 10 was drilled initially with a nine-inch and then a six-inch diameter rotary drill in November 1969, when evidence was found of cavities or loose soil zones within the overburden at 140 to 145 feet and at 160 to 165 feet. Bedrock was found at 181 feet depth, which is about six feet lower in elevation than the bedrock surface surrounding the Money Pit. During drilling into the bedrock at 10X, a cavity was found at a depth of 230 to 233 feet — fifty-one to fifty-four feet below the bedrock surface. After the drilling was completed, a six-inch diameter steel casing was installed. During clean-out of the casing, metal fragments were recovered. Because of the drilling method used, the depth at which these fragments were encountered could not be determined accurately, but it was estimated that they came from a depth of about 165 feet or higher. Down-hole blasting was carried out from 185 to 235 feet.

The six-inch casing mentioned above was installed to a depth of 188 feet and thus was embedded about seven feet into bedrock. At this point, further drilling below 188 feet was carried out by churn drilling procedures, which ground up the rock encountered, and then a process of bailing removed the ground-up rock. During this procedure, fourteen down-hole dynamite blasts were set off over a depth range of about 216 to 236 feet, with each blast followed by churn drilling and bailing to recover the displaced and ground-up rock. The main objective of the blasting was to dislodge and break presumed chests of gold coins and other treasure so that such artifacts could be recovered in the bailing apparatus. Such recovery of artifacts did not happen, but a large quantity of ground-up rock was removed. The end result of this extensive program was the creation of the controversial 10X cavity, the configuration of which is shown in Figure 25, based on accurate side look sonar measurements made by Bill Parkin in 1973. The depth range of the cavity (217 to 238 feet) is exactly coincident with the layers of gypsum with soil infillings encountered from 217.2 to 238.2 feet in Golder Hole 202, put down in 1970 beside Borehole 10 (see Figure 25 for details). These layers are quite susceptible to breakup under the effects of down-hole blasting compared to the more resistant, sound anhydrite below 238 feet and above 212 feet.

Before getting back to the exceptional story of Borehole 10, it is of considerable interest to discuss an unusual recovery of metal pieces which occurred at a depth of 84.5 to 86.5 feet in Golder Borehole 201, put down in late May 1970 and located one hundred feet north-north-east of Borehole 10X. The metal pieces were embedded in an intact 1½-inch diameter sample of sand and thus were definitely from that specific depth. This finding was so unusual that some credence was given to the possibility that the metal pieces were the remnants of an historic meteor impact during the glacial period. However, based on subsequent testing, the samples were described by The Steel Company of Canada in their report dated November 19, 1970, as friable fragments of wrought iron dating prior to 1800. This surprising discovery may be related to the original depositors. Triton Alliance put down a hole four feet from Borehole 201 to further investigate the zone where metal fragments were found. This hole (201X) was drilled in November and early December 1970 and 25½-inch diameter casing was installed to seventy-eight feet, with an open hole from seventy-eight to eighty-eight feet. Martin Pickford went down the hole on December 6, 1970, and, based on an examination of the exposed walls below seventy-eight feet, he concluded that the hole was in virgin ground. The hole was later extended to 170 feet with no unusual findings, and then no further exploration was done by Triton at this location.

Getting back to the Borehole 10 story, the results of the six-inch diameter hole initiated a program of further investigation in this area. Golder boreholes 202 and 203 were put down beside Borehole 10 in June 1970, with wood and metal fragments being recovered at about 150 feet depth. Triton then decided to enlarge the hole as was done at 201X and to designate the enlarged hole as Borehole 10X. The hole in the overburden was advanced with a twenty-seven-inch diameter casing in January and February 1971. During clean-out of the casing, pieces of chain, metal fragments, chunks of cement and pieces of wire were recovered from a depth of about 165 feet or higher. As before, the drilling method precluded accurate determination of the depth at which these artifacts were encountered.

The pieces of chain (photo 26), the metal fragments (photo 27) and the wire recovered from Borehole 10X were sent to The Steel Company of Canada for analysis, and a report dated March 30, 1971, was issued. The chain was indicated to be case-hardened steel possibly dating prior to 1750. The metal fragments were described as "folded wrought iron, and were, in all probability, produced prior to 1750." The pieces of drawn wire could not be dated and the report points out that "wire has been drawn for nearly 10,000 years."

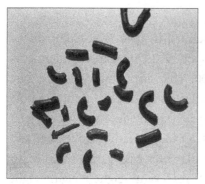 

Photo 26 — Pieces of chain from above 165 feet recovered during drilling in 1971 at Borehole 10X; largest piece at top is 1¼ inches across.

Photo 27 – Bits of metal recovered from above 165 feet during drilling in 1971 at Borehole 10X; two largest pieces at bottom are one inch long.

Two pieces of cement, one of which had a flat, rust-stained surface, were sent some years later to the Belleville Research Laboratory of Canada Cement Lafarge for examination and testing. Their report dated March 14, 1977, included test results on the cement particles and the rust flakes, and made the following statements:

> Although it is difficult to be absolutely sure, it is likely that these materials reflect human activity involving crude lime but not Portland cement. These conclusions are based on the preponderance of calcite ($CaCO_3$) in the 1 cm thick paste of Sample #1 and the extreme fineness of the calcite crystals.... This sample was not a mortar but more likely a hydrated lime which was completely carbonated.... It is likely that the lime was burned from limestone which contained quartz and other materials as impurities.... Furthermore the presence of rust at a flat surface as in sample #2, indicates contact with a man-made iron object.

The wood, metal and cement encountered in Hole 10X and Borehole

201, and the results of the testing on these materials, are all indicative of underground activity in the overburden to depths of up to 150 feet.

The twenty-seven-inch diameter casing in 10X was advanced to the bedrock surface at a depth of 181 feet. The hole in the bedrock was also enlarged to twenty-seven inches in diameter to the top of the cavity and was left uncased. In addition a twenty-seven-inch diameter hole in bedrock was extended to a depth of seven feet below the floor of the cavity, and then from a depth of seven to twenty-six feet in twenty-inch diameter, to act as a sump for pumping (see center panel of Figure 25). The drilling in bedrock was done with a churn drill and was completed by the end of July 1971. As a result, a large vertical hole in bedrock, probably of irregular shape due to the churn drilling procedure, extended below the floor of the cavity when later observations were made by an underwater television camera in August 1971. The objective was then to dewater the cavity by pumping so that observations could be made by remote camera or by sending a man down the hole. Dewatering attempts were unsuccessful in completely lowering the water level but resulted in the removal of a considerable amount of silt and mud. Sea water was pumped out, which suggested a hydraulic connection with the Money Pit, with the sea directly, or possibly both. Since the cavity could not be dewatered, an underwater television camera operated by Jim Knowles was lowered into the bedrock cavity in August 1971. The images from the cavity were displayed on the television monitor and still photos of the monitor were taken. The *Chronicle-Herald* of November 23, 1971, reported on the sensational findings as follows:

> A series of pictures show faint outlines of what project manager Dan Blankenship says he is certain are three chests, one having a handle on the end and a curved top. Beside another of the chests or boxes, he says, is some sort of tool, not unlike a pick-axe.

> Another view clearly shows three logs lying on the floor of

the chamber, more than 40 feet deeper than any previous treasure seekers had ever explored, Mr. Blankenship said.

A more gruesome revelation by the camera probing the same cell was the appearance on the monitor of a human hand, partly clenched, suspended in water, Mr. Blankenship said.

Startled by what he saw, Mr. Blankenship said he summoned all his workers, one by one, into the shack housing the television monitor. Each man confirmed that the hand, still covered with flesh, had what looked like a slash mark across the back, while below the mark the mangled flesh suggested it had been torn or chopped from wrist, he said.

Blankenship told the reporter that he had sought the advice of experts who told him that under certain conditions it would be possible for human flesh to be preserved, especially if it had been embedded in clay, such as is found at great depths on Oak Island. Drilling could have caused the hand to break loose in the water.

A second session with an underwater television camera provided by CBC Halifax in August 1971 recorded images of the cavity at 10X. The film was inferred by Triton to show chests, timbers and tools as well as two tunnels leading from the cavity.

The next step by Triton Alliance was to send a diver down Borehole 10X to explore the cavity. For this purpose it was necessary to lower the water level, by pumping from adjacent dewatering holes, from its static depth of about forty-three feet below ground surface to a depth of about one hundred feet or more, so that the water pressure on the diver would be less than 140 feet. At about 180 feet during the first diving attempt, water rushed in below the cased hole so fast that it was sweeping the mask from the diver's face. The flow of water was reduced

Photo 28 — Aerial view of Oak Island in 1986. Money Pit is at circular area to left of buildings; Cave-in Pit is at right of buildings.

for subsequent dives when Blankenship, Triton's field manager, bull-dozed soil into the sea where it was thought the entrance to the flood tunnel was located. This observation, and the general lowering of the water level in other shafts and wells during pumping from Borehole 10X, indicated a widespread underground communication of water in the bedrock.

More than ten dives to the cavity in 10X were made in 1971 and 1972. The *Chronicle-Herald* reported on one such event on December 7, 1971. Diver Phil Irwin told the reporter that he could not see any walls, only a ghostly ceiling having eight or ten "V" shaped gouges extending upward. Reflection of his light on the ceiling in certain spots resembled a fluorescent light. He could not see bottom (through the water) although he was standing on it. Also, it was assumed that the rock cavern, which was initially five to seven feet high, had become fif-teen feet high where it had been penetrated by Borehole 10X, due to the falling away of rock from the roof of the cavern. However, this is not the correct interpretation of how the cavity was formed. As indicated previously, it is certain that the cavity was already fully formed by the drilling and blasting carried out in late 1969. This is completely contrary to the understanding at that time that the cavity in the bedrock was mined out by original depositors to secure their treasure.

Other divers in 1972 reported that the walls of the cavity could be readily touched on three sides. Nothing was found during the diving inspections to confirm the dramatic observations drawn from the television cameras of a severed hand and chests with bodies draped across them. It has been speculated that the floating hand seen by Dan Blankenship on the TV monitor was a workman's glove, which could easily have dropped into the hole. Based on careful examination of the 10X video, and taking into account the limited movement patterns of the underwater camera, it is readily concluded that the horizontal tunnel or tunnels inferred on the second filming were merely different views of the vertical churn-drilled hole extending below the floor of the cavity. The divers had difficulty with visibility and their efforts proved unsuccessful in finding hard evidence of man-made workings in the rock cavern. The conclusion is inescapable that the 10X cavity was formed by the drilling and blasting in late 1969 and was not the product of the original depositors.

In view of the absence of specific finds in the bedrock cavern at Borehole 10X and subsequent skepticism with regard to the validity of the television images from the underwater camera, attention was focused on the interesting artifacts found in the overburden above about 165 feet depth in Borehole 10X, and on whether or not artifacts occurred elsewhere. A series of boreholes were drilled in 1973 and one of them, located 660 feet north of the Money Pit, recovered a piece of wire at 110 feet. The wire was indicated by The Steel Company of Canada in their report dated June 11, 1973, as being typical of wire drawn from the sixteenth to the nineteenth century. This span of about three hundred years does little to identify the exact period during which the original work was carried out.

A twelve- by six-foot shaft put down in late 1973 and early 1974 at this location became known as the Triton Shaft (see Figure 22). It was abandoned at one hundred feet due to lack of funds, terminating just ten feet short of the depth at which the wire was found. No clues were

Photo 29 — Causeway and south side of Oak Island, 1998.

Photo 30 — Smith's Cove looking toward Borehole 10X at building, 1998.

Photo 31 — Money Pit enclosed by fence looking northeast toward buildings at Borehole 10X; the borehole is at building to left of cars, 1998.

Photo 32 — Looking west-northwest along South Shore Cove from flood-ed pit; former stone triangle was located within pit limits, 1998.

discovered about the wire and the reason for its presence at such great depth, and so distant from the Money Pit and Flood Tunnel.

From 1975 to 1977, further drilling and investigation work was car-ried out, but no substantial information was recovered. In 1976, Dan Blankenship narrowly escaped being trapped in the twenty-seven-inch diameter casing of Borehole 10X when it collapsed at ninety-five feet depth. From 1978 to 1980, Blankenship embarked on an ambitious and innovative venture to excavate a large diameter shaft at Borehole 10X in the hope of finding a route to the treasure at a depth of about 165 feet, where artifacts were recovered from the first work. The top fifty feet of the shaft was lined with eight-foot diameter steel casings of ½-inch plate recovered from old railway tank cars. From fifty to ninety-one feet the shaft was lined with welded steel plate internally braced. Below ninety-one feet, the shaft was advanced in sections and lined with concrete. The work was difficult and was stopped at 126 feet, well above the depths of interest, which according to Dan Blankenship were from 140 to 145 feet and from 150 to 165 feet. The Borehole 10X project was put aside for six years. From 1987 to 1990 the concrete-lined shaft at Borehole 10X was advanced to the bedrock surface at 181 feet, and no evidence of tunnels, artifacts or treasure was found. In view of the previous findings in over-burden in the six-inch and twenty-seven-inch casings, this represents a significant inconsistency that cannot be readily explained.

In 1983 a deep exploratory drill-hole (No. 401) was put down about two hundred feet north of the Money Pit (see Figure 22). The findings determined the thickness of the anhydrite bedrock below the soil lay-ers. This hole encountered hard glacial till to 181 feet, anhydrite bed-rock from 181 to 360 feet and grey slate bedrock from 360 to 590 feet, at which depth the hole was terminated.

One of the more baffling observations of this period was made in the winter of 1987, when four circular holes were observed in the ice about five hundred feet off South Shore. The holes were about fifteen to forty feet in diameter and spaced at about 150 feet (see Figure 22). The water depth in this area is about fifteen to twenty feet at low tide. The same configura-tion of ice holes had been observed previously in February 1980, when they had been attributed to circulation of warmer water from beneath Oak Island to this offshore area. The interpretation of Triton Alliance was that the ice hole locations were at the inlet to the assumed lower flood tunnel connecting South Shore to the Money Pit. The 1941 dye tests of Edwin Hamilton had indicated a discharge point about three hundred feet offshore, in water depths of about fifteen feet at low tide, proving a direct connection with the Money Pit. This point was in the vicinity where the ice holes had appeared. Therefore it was assumed that the similarity of the two observations confirmed the presence of an underwater inlet to a lower flood tunnel, one which supplemented that linking the Money Pit to Smith's Cove. No consideration was given to the possibility that continued pumping on the island may have created a network of solution passages within the underlying water-soluble bedrock. As explained in Chapter 7, these pervious zones in the anhydrite form the underground water flow system between the Money Pit and the South Shore.

In 1987 Triton made plans for 'The Big Dig.' The engineering approach for this venture, described in the report by Bill Cox of Cox Underground Research, was to excavate an eighty-foot diameter lined shaft at the Money Pit and to extend the shaft some 220 feet to the wood-lined cavern in bedrock previously identified by drilling. Water would be pumped from four pumping stations to facilitate the excavation. The proposed configuration of the shaft with respect to the Money Pit and Borehole 10X is shown on Figure 26 (see also Figure 22). The plan included a cofferdam at Smith's Cove (further offshore than the previous Triton cofferdam) to prevent water from entering the Flood Tunnel, and a huge cofferdam at South Shore Cove to prevent water from entering the assumed flood tunnel(s) at this location.

The entrance of the presumed flood tunnel(s) at South Shore was assumed to be five hundred feet offshore, coincident with the ice hole locations. The cofferdam required to isolate this area would have been about two thousand feet long and would have involved about two hundred thousand cubic yards of fill. The unusual situation at the proposed South Shore cofferdam was recognized by Bill Cox, who stated in a letter dated September 22, 1987, to David Tobias of Triton: "The location of those 'damned' ice holes is astounding. They are so far offshore that a cofferdam is probably impractical." Not surprisingly, the proposed $10-million 'Big Dig' did not proceed due to insufficient financing.

At this point in the search for treasure, a considerable amount of drill-hole data to great depths was available, including Borehole 401 extending to a depth of 590 feet. This allowed a reasonable understanding of the overall geological conditions at Oak Island to be developed, as illustrated by the geological section on Figure 27. This shows a thick layer of anhydrite, which is known to include varying thicknesses of gypsum and limestone, overlying the hard, resistant slate bedrock that is dominant throughout the region. Above the bedrock is a thick sequence of glacial till, generally of a hard, clayey nature.

Since the proposal for 'The Big Dig,' Triton Alliance pursued a number of detection studies in the early 1990s involving detailed geophysical investigations at the Money Pit and a detailed groundwater

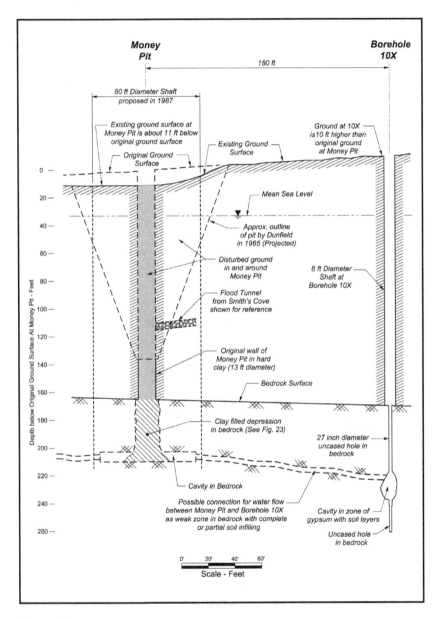

Figure 26

Section Showing 80-Foot Diameter Shaft Proposed in 1987 with Respect to the Money Pit and Borehole 10X

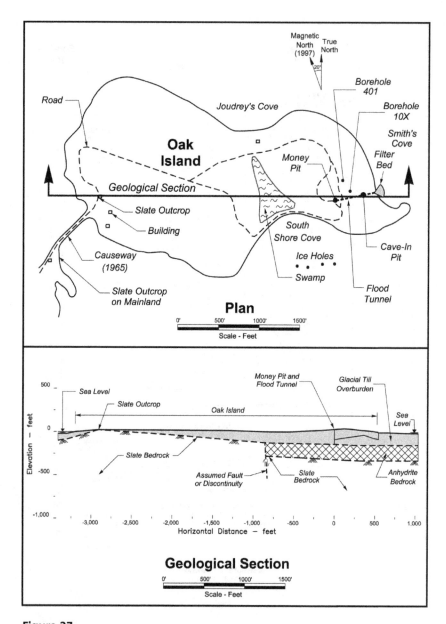

Figure 27

Geological Section of Oak Island

and bathymetry study by the Woods Hole Oceanographic Institution in 1995. However, these studies did not crack the shell of mystery surrounding the Oak Island enigma.

In 1996 a government-sponsored survey was made in the water surrounding Oak Island to determine the exact configuration of the sea bottom. The results of this work were published as *Geological Survey of Canada Open File 3610*, issued in April 1998. The report includes a colour-coded 'image' of the sea bottom configuration. One of the findings was the presence of a number of depressions in the seabed at South Shore Cove. These features were interpreted as possible sinkholes or pockmarks (depressions), and some of them occur in the vicinity of the ice holes. The map did not indicate evidence of any cofferdam remnants in South Shore Cove in the same area. Another interesting feature was the possible wreck of a ship in thirty-five feet of water at a location about two thousand feet south of the island.

Two more recent attempts to resolve the mystery are of interest. In 1999 and again in 2001, Ron Aston of Noon Star Ltd., Kitty Hawk, North Carolina, and a group of supporters drilled about forty holes to depths from thirty to fifty feet on the ridge north of the Money Pit. The objective of the investigation was to search for an offset chamber containing the spoils from the sack of Havana in 1762. The holes encountered natural soils, and no evidence of any offset chambers was found.

Fred Nolan believed that the huge boulders, weighing some twenty to forty tons each, located within Lots 9 to 14, which he owned at that time, formed a man-made Christian cross (see Figure 22). He made these findings public in 1992, creating much speculation as to their meaning. However, boulder terrains abound across Nova Scotia, covering a wide swath of territory, and the presence of huge boulders on Oak Island should come as no surprise, for the island is a drumlin, a geological feature formed during the Ice Age. The boulders are merely glacial erratics dumped during the retreat of the ice sheets. Nevertheless, some amusing theories have been advanced.

In 2005 a new group entered the stage for the treasure search at Oak Island. Several partners of Rock Management Group Ltd., Traverse City, Michigan (an oil and gas venture) purchased the Oak Island interests of David Tobias, Montreal. The new group, commonly referred to as the Michigan Group, entered into an agreement with Dan Blankenship for further exploration and scientific studies. Unfortunately, there was considerable delay in approvals by the Nova Scotia government of the application for renewal of the Treasure Trove License. However, the Treasure Trove License was renewed in early 2012 and exploration activities are under way. The Michigan Group plans to use a scientific approach to solve the Oak Island Mystery and may have success where others have failed.

The pursuit of treasure on Oak Island has taken many twists and turns over the past 220 years, since the discovery of the Money Pit in 1795. Each band of treasure-seekers attracted to the island has had to penetrate to ever-increasing depths (see Figure 28). A different line of investigation adopted in the search for treasure on the island has been the attempt to discover chambers, or similar facilities, significantly offset from the Money Pit itself. These various searches have extended the length and breadth of the island. As far as is known, no treasure has been recovered, but artifacts have been found that provide evidence of human activity on the island prior to 1795.

There exist a number of theories, and a great amount of speculation, pertaining to offset chambers and why these should have been used to cache treasure at shallow depth, where it was more readily retrievable, rather than at depth within the Money Pit. Current literature on Oak Island reviews many of these theories (see References). The incontrovertible evidence of a Flood Tunnel linking the Money Pit to Smith's Cove and the presence of iron and wood-lined cavities within the bedrock at the Money Pit suggest that an enormous amount of effort was expended on Oak Island. The magnitude of this effort, at a significant depth below bedrock surface in the Money Pit, is unlikely to have been made for the purpose of providing a 'decoy,' as has been ventured from time to time by the advocates of offset chambers.

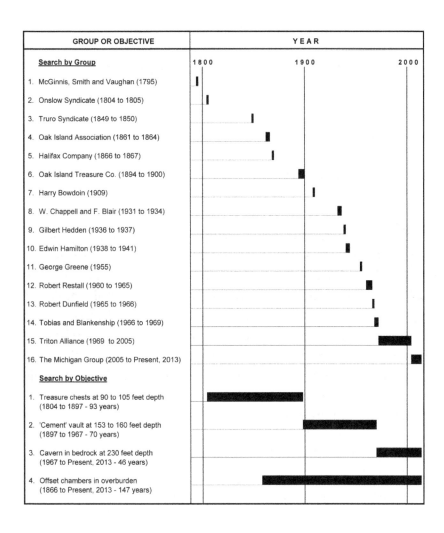

GROUP OR OBJECTIVE	YEAR		
Search by Group	1800	1900	2000
1. McGinnis, Smith and Vaughan (1795)			
2. Onslow Syndicate (1804 to 1805)			
3. Truro Syndicate (1849 to 1850)			
4. Oak Island Association (1861 to 1864)			
5. Halifax Company (1866 to 1867)			
6. Oak Island Treasure Co. (1894 to 1900)			
7. Harry Bowdoin (1909)			
8. W. Chappell and F. Blair (1931 to 1934)			
9. Gilbert Hedden (1936 to 1937)			
10. Edwin Hamilton (1938 to 1941)			
11. George Greene (1955)			
12. Robert Restall (1960 to 1965)			
13. Robert Dunfield (1965 to 1966)			
14. Tobias and Blankenship (1966 to 1969)			
15. Triton Alliance (1969 to 2005)			
16. The Michigan Group (2005 to Present, 2013)			
Search by Objective			
1. Treasure chests at 90 to 105 feet depth (1804 to 1897 - 93 years)			
2. 'Cement' vault at 153 to 160 feet depth (1897 to 1967 - 70 years)			
3. Cavern in bedrock at 230 feet depth (1967 to Present, 2013 - 46 years)			
4. Offset chambers in overburden (1866 to Present, 2013 - 147 years)			

Figure 28

Chronology of Search for Oak Island Treasure by Group and Objective

CHAPTER 7

A Theory Evolves

Now what I want is, Facts. Facts alone are wanted
in life. Plant nothing else, and root out everything
else. Stick to Facts, Sir.
      Mr. Gradgrind in "Hard Times" (Dickens)

Facts are essential to support any credible hypothesis. Sometimes such facts are difficult to establish when supporting evidence is either unreliable or contradictory. It is this lack of incontrovertible fact that has fuelled speculation regarding the nature of the workings on Oak Island, and added to their mystique. Nevertheless, there are important clues of a technical nature that enable development of a credible theory consistent with failure to regain access to the underground workings of the Money Pit. This theory is based on the premise that the Flood Tunnel was not part of the original excavation project.

The technical evidence does not give a reliable date for the original excavation of the Money Pit shaft and the works at Smith's Cove. The axe head discovered in the Chappell Shaft (Shaft No. 21) in 1931, and identified as being of a type in use from the early 1700s to the early 1800s, gives a wide range of possible dates. The analysis of a piece of brass from the Money Pit and wrought iron artifacts from Smith's Cove indicates a date prior to about 1800–1850, but does not provide a reasonable limit on the early side of the time range. On the other hand, available evidence suggests that the works at Smith's Cove date to a period of about 1700 to 1800. The carbon dating cannot be used with any degree of certainty, as the range in dates is understandably very wide, varying between about 1550 and 1850.

It is certain that the originators of the Money Pit were in total ignorance of the potentially hazardous undertaking they commenced when they began to dig a shaft to bedrock on the island. Unlike other islands in the vicinity, Oak Island is characterised by a thick mantle of glacial till overlying a water-soluble anhydrite bedrock. These important geological features must be given some detailed attention.

First, the hard, impermeable nature of the glacial till made it highly favourable for excavation of shafts and tunnels with a minimum of timbering and other supports, despite its extensive thickness. However, where more pervious sandy zones occur locally at depth in the glacial till, excavation is difficult, as demonstrated by the water inflow, and sometimes bottom failure, experienced at Shafts 15 to 19 in 1898–99. Second, excavation in anhydrite bedrock is positively dangerous as anhydrite is exceedingly soluble, more so in salt water than in fresh, and the diggings extended to well below sea level.

One important characteristic of anhydrite is that it absorbs water to form gypsum and in the process expands sometimes up to about 63 per cent by volume, with consequent shearing and development of fractured zones. Anhydrite is renowned for producing problem situations in tunnelling and foundation works. More than one engineering project has fallen foul of highly sheared anhydrite rock, with water in abundance flowing through the solution channels that frequently accompany these zones. Out of all the islands along the seaboard of Nova Scotia, it was a singular misfortune that Oak Island was selected for the digging of the Money Pit, since the water-soluble and cavity-prone nature of the anhydrite bedrock underlying the island is the most important feature of the island's geology responsible for the loss of the original Money Pit shaft.

The instructions given to the original diggers were probably quite simple and could have been, for example, "dig a shaft to bedrock and make a chamber in the rock." The considerable depth to bedrock (167 feet) likely surprised those early diggers. Oak platforms were installed at ten-foot stages to facilitate access for personnel and equipment, as they would not have been required for support of the Money Pit walls in the hard, impermeable glacial till. However, such support may have been required if the diggers encountered the sandy, more pervious glacial till as the bedrock surface was approached. It is assumed that the original diggers were able to cope with the conditions encountered, which must have been more favourable than those found at other locations by the treasure-seekers of 1898–99. We estimate that digging from shaft to bedrock would have taken a crew of sturdy men (probably seafarers) no longer than three to four months to complete, though sinews might have been strained on occasion. Considering the depth achieved, it is likely that ventilation by furnace was used.

The most interesting, and possibly the most controversial part of the shaft excavation would have been the section that penetrated rock to a final depth of about 210 feet below ground surface. It is natural to ask how the first diggers could accomplish such a feat when later searchers, with more modern tools and equipment, failed. There is a perfectly reasonable explanation. The anhydrite bedrock is infested with soil-filled cavities, as has been proven by the various deep-drilling programs carried out. The bedrock and the soil-filled cavities were subjected to the tremendous pressure of ice accumulated on the land during glacial times more than ten thousand years ago. Since that consolidation, these soil-filled cavities were not subject to any significant erosive effects of migrating groundwater until man first penetrated them, initiating a pattern of seepage within the water soluble rock by his pumping activities. This new seepage pattern, radiating outwards from the base of the Money Pit, would progressively enlarge as pumping continued, by dissolving the anhydrite and eroding the soil contained within any soil-filled cavities.

It is speculated that the toiling diggers would have been thrilled to find that Mother Nature had provided virtually ready-made chambers in which to store their hoard of treasure. All they would have needed to do was to remove the soil from the cavities they had stumbled across, possibly enlarging them by some nominal rock excavation, the anhydrite

being relatively soft compared to most types of rock. Some bulkhead-
ing might have been required in conjunction with timbering to support
the roof. The presence of timbers in the roof of one such chamber (see
Figure 23) testifies to the necessity for support in this rather weak material. It is possible also that some support measures were incorporated
into the shaft section that penetrated the bedrock. Some minor water
seepage was certainly experienced, and caulking of the most obvious
water-bearing fissures is likely to have been implemented. In view of
the substantial quantity of treasure requiring stowage, several treasure
chambers were likely excavated, all radiating from the bottom of the
shaft or in close proximity. This phase of the work would have taken
only about one or two months. Overall, the period required to excavate
the Money Pit shaft and its treasure chambers in bedrock is unlikely to
have been greater than four to six months from start to finish.

It is virtually certain that some type of failure in the underground
workings prevented recovery of the treasure, though a degree of
uncertainty must exist as to the specific nature of the failure mechanism involved. The actual mode of failure might well have involved a
combination of circumstances, which at this late date are impossible to
define with assurance, but two scenarios represent the extreme limits
of a wide range of possibilities.

The first scenario assumes that the treasure was cached safely below
ground with little difficulty. Ingress of water into the workings was
manageable and, for all intents and purposes, the rock exposed was
stable. A clay seal was possibly installed at the base of the shaft, which
would explain the clay-filled depression in the rock deduced from
recent drilling. The shaft was then covered over or sealed at the surface
and allowed to fill with water. This process would have enlarged and
extended the systemic seepage paths within the water-soluble rock.
Further enlargement of these seepage paths would have been initiated
as soon as bailing or pumping began in order to retrieve the treasure.
Therefore, the failure mechanism in this scenario is one of increased
seepage during the bailing process. However, some rock-slabbing of

the walls and roof to the treasure chambers could well have ensued in a progressive manner. This could well have threatened the overall stability of the workings themselves. What is certain is that the process of dewatering the underground chambers would enlarge the fissures within the anhydrite by solution. Eventually a point would have been reached when bailing, or pumping, would have been unable to cope with the rate of inflow of subterranean water. It is likely that this point was reached before the water could be drawn down to the level of the treasure chamber, and the treasure would not have been recovered.

The second scenario suggests a catastrophic failure of the rock within which the treasure chambers were excavated. This would likely have taken the form of a major roof collapse, or a blow-out if the external hydrostatic pressure exceeded the rock strength. Such sudden, violent and dramatic failures have been known to cause great loss of life underground. Though of rare occurrence, the phenomenon is well documented in the practice of mine engineering. The consequent surge of debris into the workings and up the shaft would have plugged the lower section, and any attempt at recovery of men, materials or treasure entombed underground would have proved fruitless.

Following the 1795 discovery of the Money Pit, treasure hunters would progressively enlarge the seepage paths within the soluble bedrock by their pumping activities. Also, large amounts of soil would have been eroded from the initially soil-filled cavities, resulting in the voids encountered in various drill-holes penetrating the anhydrite bedrock.

The presence of cavities within the anhydrite thus constitutes a network of solution channels beneath the island, whereby sea water is drawn towards the Money Pit when pumping is in progress (see Figure 29). The evidence provided by dye tests (1941), ice holes (1987) and the Geological Survey of Canada map (1998), supports the conclusion that small sinkholes exist in the seabed off South Shore, and these are the result of prolonged pumping.

There has always been some doubt about the true location of the

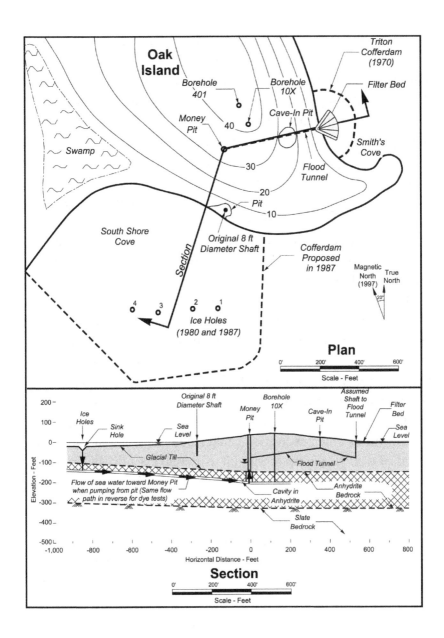

Figure 29

Flow System from South Shore to Money Pit

original Money Pit shaft. Some of the old reference drawings show that it is about fifteen to twenty feet north-northwest of the generally presumed location shown on the various figures in this book. It is possible that this confusion arises because there were two original shafts, one being the Money Pit shaft and the other being an offset shaft excavated during pre-1795 attempts to recover the treasure in the years immediately following its loss. These attempts at the Money Pit may have resulted in the complex timber, cement and iron occurences identified from about 120 to 160 feet by various drilling programs, including the timber/cement structure at 153 to 160 feet. Even the clay-filled depression in bedrock could have been an attempt to seal the bottom of the shaft so that excavation could then be carried out through it. Based on present knowledge, such an approach would be doomed to failure.

Once realisation had set in that it was hopeless to recover the lost treasure, a plan was made to ensure that it was never recovered by anyone else. This involved the construction of the well-known Flood Tunnel, the presence of which has severely hindered the various treasure-seeking operations on the island. It is considered highly significant that the connection between the Flood Tunnel and the Money Pit shaft occurs at 110 to 114 feet below ground surface: the approximate depth to which excavation could readily be achieved with a soil (puddled clay) plug in the Money Pit to prevent extensive boiling up of water from the depths of the anhydrite bedrock. This phase of the work would have required miners and other trades with particular skills in maintaining the grade of tunnels, working in confined conditions, providing reliable ventilation underground, constructing an offshore cofferdam and having knowledge of filter design for construction of the inlet works. Therefore, it must be concluded that this phase probably lasted between eighteen months and two years.

It is of interest to speculate on the reason why the Money Pit was linked with Smith's Cove, rather than to South Shore Cove, approximately 150 feet closer in distance. The diggings of Dunfield and Blankenship in 1965–66, revealing an original shaft on South Shore, suggest that the miners involved in the construction of the Flood Tunnel probably commenced their tunnelling there before changing to Smith's Cove. The presence of five feet of boulders at a depth of eighty-five to ninety feet is highly suggestive of an unsuccessful attempt to stabilise the base of a shaft experiencing quicksand conditions.

The excavation of the Money Pit shaft was a simple affair compared to that of the Flood Tunnel. It required little mining skill and could have been achieved by a ship's crew. There is no suggestion in this initial phase of any official sanction or involvement. The excavation of the Flood Tunnel and its allied works was a different matter. Official sponsorship of this phase is likely to have been necessary, due to the amount of time required to execute the work and the need for experienced labour and materials. This sponsorship is likely to have been provided by the British government, in view of the clauses contained within the Shoreham Grant of 1759, and is likely to have occurred between 1752 and 1754. The similarity of the Flood Tunnel to British military tunnels of the eighteenth century, and the engineers and troops likely involved in its excavation, together with the construction of the ancillary works, will be considered in Chapter 11.

Excavation of the Flood Tunnel from the Money Pit toward Smith's Cove would have been carried out from a timber working platform at about the 120-foot depth. After completing the Flood Tunnel, the Money Pit shaft from 120 feet up to 105 feet was filled with a puddled-clay seal, after which decoy treasure was placed between platforms at 105 feet and ninety-eight feet (see Figure 30).

Allowing for a sea level rise of one foot per century and a construction period from 1752 to 1754, the filter bed at Smith's Cove would have been built at a time when sea level was about 2½ feet lower than it is today. Based on our present knowledge of the filter system location (see Figures 13 and 24), it appears that the feeder drains started somewhat above the low tide level that prevailed at the time of construction. The clever design of the flood system did not require the drains to extend to low tide level since the filter bed and Flood Tunnel

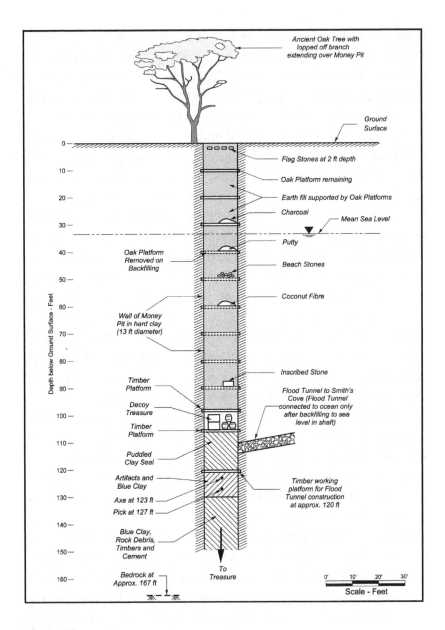

Figure 30

Money Pit at End of Second Phase Construction to Excavate the Flood Tunnel and Place the Decoy Treasure

system would be charged during the high tide cycle, the water stored in the system being more than adequate to feed the Money Pit during periods of low tide. The engineers of the Flood Tunnel thereby created a most effective water trap, which served to frustrate treasure recovery attempts in later years. The gradual rise in sea level over the years merely made the flood trap more effective.

One of the final acts in construction of the Flood Tunnel and inlet works would have been to breach the cofferdam. This must have been perversely satisfying for the military engineers engaged on the work, and would have taken place after the Money Pit had been backfilled at least to sea level.

Evidence of clandestine activity at the Money Pit was bound to be discovered sooner or later. Therefore, it is postulated that some decoy treasure would have been provided, but its value would have been minimal in relation to that which remained deep underground. Based on available evidence, the decoy treasure was placed between two timber platforms, marginally above the intersection with the Flood Tunnel (see Figure 30). The designers of the ingenious trap intended that the decoy treasure be recovered, the water trap being sprung only if deeper digging was carried out. The abundant supply of water entering the works via the Flood Tunnel would have discouraged further exploration of the Money Pit. However, the trap was first sprung in 1804 by the Onslow Group when their shaft was just five feet short of the upper timber platform covering the decoy treasure. After they laid down their tools in respect of the Sabbath, they returned to find the workings flooded. The decoy treasure was put further out of reach as a consequence of the collapse of the undermined platforms that occurred in 1861.

The stone triangle was clearly an 'out of the way' marker or arrow toward the Money Pit, probably placed during the first phase of the work. The various drilled stones probably served as survey control markers during construction of the Flood Tunnel. There is no reference in the early records of the search to obvious mounds of soil remaining from the extensive earthworks carried out, and it is probable that spoil materials from the excavations were spread out or dumped offshore. Also, it is likely that most of the offshore cofferdam in Smith's Cove was dismantled. Thus the site was cleaned-up prior to abandonment, leaving little trace of human activity. Was the stone triangle left in place because its removal was overlooked, or was it left intentionally? We cannot tell, but bearing in mind the intensive activity carried out on the island, possibly spanning several decades, it is surprising that a larger number of artifacts and other remains have not been found.

The overwhelming conclusion that emerges from the reconstruction of likely events that led to the loss of the Money Pit, and its subsequent cover up, is that it was a rash gamble right from the start. If it had not been for the peculiar geology of Oak Island, it might well have succeeded. Since it is human nature to mask failure, if at all possible, and especially where it is severely embarrassing, it is not surprising that there is a lack of corroborative detail regarding exactly what went on at Oak Island. If the gamble had paid off, and the treasure had been safely recovered, no doubt the history books would be full of the exploits of those responsible. As Sir Winston Churchill said, "ambition, not so much for vulgar ends, but for fame, glints in every mind."

The first diggings at the site of the Money Pit are unlikely to have been made before 1665, since this was the year in which knowledge of furnace-driven ventilation began to be disseminated; neither could the final phase have been accomplished later than 1759, the year of the Shoreham Grant. This time frame is one of substantial and increasing trade across the Atlantic as the European powers expanded and consolidated their possessions in the New World, often in violent confrontation. Honest merchantmen had little defence against more powerful adversaries, whether they were pirates or privateers of rival nations. It is surprising that despite such hazards vast volumes of goods were safely transported: furs from Canada, fish from Newfoundland, timber and tobacco from New England, sugar and rum from the West Indies and, of course, gold, silver and precious stones from New Spain.

CHAPTER 8

A Brief History Lesson

I am a part of all that I have met;
Yet all experience is an arch wherethro'
Gleams that untravelled world
　　　　　　　"Ulysses" (Tennyson)

The review of the historical record of the various diggings on Oak Island has concluded that the most likely period during which the first excavations were made by the originators of the Money Pit is towards the end of the seventeenth century. It is useful, therefore, to briefly review the history of the region with a view to establishing the backdrop against which the excavation of the Money Pit would likely have been carried out. It is hoped that the account given herein will help those readers, unaware of the violent past of this vast region, to appreciate the turbulent events that characterized the period. Figure 31 illustrates the key locations in Acadia referred to in this discourse.

Following the celebrated landing of Cabot on these shores in 1497, more than a century elapsed before Europeans showed any real interest in the region. In 1604, Henry IV of France awarded Sieur de Monts a commission "to people and cultivate said lands, search for gold and silver, build forts and towns, and grant lands." Four vessels departed from France on April 7, 1604, under the joint commands of de Monts, Jean de Poutrincourt and Samuel de Champlain. On May 16, 1604, three of these ships put into the harbour now known as Liverpool. There de Monts was surprised to find an adventurous fellow-countryman, Rossignol, trading fur with the natives. De Monts, with callous disregard for Rossignol's welfare, confiscated his vessel, goods, supplies and equipment and abandoned him to his fate in the wilderness. It is an ironic

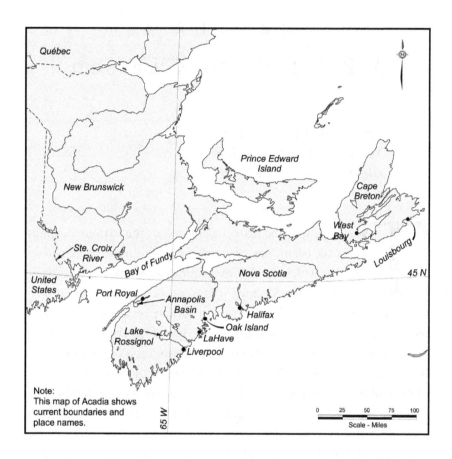

Figure 31

Map of Acadia

testimony to Rossignol that the largest lake in the area is named in his memory.

De Monts removed his party westwards and penetrated into the Bay of Fundy, venturing into the Annapolis Basin. Their explorations lasted the entire summer season as they penetrated the numerous creeks and backwaters in the region. With the approach of winter, Poutrincourt took an early passage home and de Monts set up camp on an island at the mouth of the St. Croix River. The winter was long and bitter, wood and water were exhausted, provisions ran low and thirty-five souls (about half of the party) were to perish from scurvy and other ills. The experience of this first winter resolved the party to seek a more favourable location for settlement and, accordingly, they returned to the Annapolis Basin to found Port Royal, which was to become the bastion of French settlement in Acadia.

The first attempt at permanent settlement of Port Royal failed, and de Monts instructed Champlain to relocate to Quebec. Poutrincourt, however, was not to be dissuaded from Acadia. In 1610, he returned with a priest, Messire Jossé Flesche, who quickly set about his priestly duties. By June 1611, the population of the second settlement at Port Royal had swelled to about sixty.

In the same year Louis XIII, who had succeeded to the throne after his father's fatal stabbing, was persuaded by Poutrincourt to grant the whole province of Acadia, with the exception of Port Royal, to a very wealthy and influential noblewoman, Madame la Marquise de Gucherville, in order to secure more aid for the struggling colony. De Monts ceded his rights on the understanding that she would invest money in the region, and foster missionary activity to convert the 'heathen.'

Poutrincourt remained in France, but he dispatched a vessel to Port Royal in January 1612, which made the outbound trip in a mere twenty-three days. There were many other comings and goings, and de Gucherville lived up to her commitments by sponsoring missionary activity throughout the New World, where the French were in the ascendant. Trouble was inevitable, and in 1613 the first shots were fired in anger between the French in Acadia and the English settlers to the south. This is no surprise since hostilities between England and France had run like an open sore for centuries.

On the basis of Cabot's voyages of 1497 and 1498, the English settlers in Virginia had claimed all land to the north, including Acadia. In 1613 Captain Samuel Argall sailed into the Gulf of Maine with an armed escort to protect his fishing fleet. Argall was not noted for his scruples and appears to have relished the prospect of besieging the French. Port Royal fell after a brief and bloody battle, and half of the remnant French were permitted to sail away in their shallops, hopefully back to France. The other half were taken as prisoners to Jamestown. Though the British and the French were not at war, the governor of Virginia, Sir Thomas Dale, was so pleased with Argall's action that he dispatched Argall with more ships to make sure that Port Royal was totally destroyed.

French settlements had been temporarily cleaned out of Acadia by Argall, nevertheless there was still a considerable trade with France, with upwards of five hundred vessels trading in furs and fish along the coast. Biencourt, who had been in charge of Port Royal at the time of Argall's attack, reappeared and began rebuilding in 1618. He beseeched the authorities to establish more fortified posts in the region. Thenceforth Acadia was to become a minor battlefield.

James I of England, in 1621, granted Acadia to Sir William Alexander, one of his favourites, for colonization. Grand plans were laid, but little of a practical nature was accomplished until 1624, when an expedition was dispatched to the conquered territory. It returned without landing, bringing news that the French were back again and everywhere strongly in possession. Eventually, in 1628, five armed ships were assembled under David Kirke, who was charged to remove the French from Acadia. The ships, each captained by one of his brothers, carried disproportionately large Huguenot crews. At that time the French authorities forbade Protestants from settlement in their colonies overseas. The brutal slaughter of thirty thousand Huguenots, known as the St. Bartholomew Massacre, on August 24, 1572, was still fresh in people's memories. As a consequence there was no shortage of volunteers amidst the Huguenot refugees in England to take up arms against their erstwhile countrymen.

Port Royal fell a second time to the invading British, other French settlements were laid waste and the seas cleared of all presence of the enemy. Little was attempted by way of British colonization. The following summer David Kirke faced Champlain before Quebec, and a year later, in 1629, Champlain surrendered. Three years after this first taking of Quebec by Kirke it was handed back to the French by the Treaty of Saint Germain in 1632.

Charlevoix, writing some hundred years after Champlain's surrender to Kirke, describes the limited accomplishments of the French in the New World up to that time:

> Cape Breton at that date, 1632, was of but little importance
> — the fort at Quebec, surrounded by some inferior build-
> ings, and some sheds, two or three cabins in the Island of
> Montreal, perhaps as many more at Tadoussac and other
> places on the River St. Lawrence, the beginning of a settle-
> ment at Three Rivers, and the ruins of Port Royal — in
> these consist New France.

In 1620 a little-publicized incident took place to the south and was to have serious repercussions throughout the region. In that year the *Mayflower* landed on the rocky shores of Massachusetts and discharged one hundred brave souls who were to lay the foundation stones of hard work and free enterprise in New England. Armed only with their faith in a just God, they were to prove a bastion against French encroachment to the south. The Puritans disapproved of the return of Acadia to France in 1632, especially as the return was traded away for a queen's dowry. However, for twenty years following the Treaty of Saint Germain, the French in Acadia could rest secure.

In 1654 Cromwell, Lord Protector of England, averse to a public declaration of war with France, sent out ships to Boston, there to be reinforced and dispatched to Acadia. Soon the region was back in British hands, for the third time. English entrepreneurs Sir Thomas Temple and Charles de la Tour obtained patent rights and set out to develop Acadia. They repaired a few forts, set up regulations to control fishing and the fur trade and spent prodigious sums of money in investments in a region that they hoped would one day yield a dividend. They were never to reap that dividend. In 1658 Cromwell died, and two years later Charles II ascended the throne. In 1667 a treaty was concluded with the French at Breda whereby all the former French possessions in North America were returned to France. Sir Thomas Temple and his men were forced to yield all the forts and improvements they had made. For the third time Acadia was returned to the French for little in return.

The farming lands in Acadia were not extensive: marshes required dyking and draining in order to render them suitable for agriculture. There was no easy mineral wealth. The prospects for Acadia were not auspicious, and the close proximity of the ancient enemy to the south, with the near certainty of renewed hostility at some time, cast a gloom over this thinly settled colony of New France. The population was augmented slightly by new arrivals, but within twenty years of the signing of the Treaty of Breda the total European population of Acadia was still less than one thousand, and that of New France less than six thousand all told. This small group, scattered throughout the vast region in tiny settlements, managed to remain detached from much of the armed conflict that prevailed.

In 1675 an aboriginal American, known to the English as King Philip, organised certain tribes in southern Massachusetts and Rhode Island. They made a concerted effort to drive the English back into the sea. They failed, and King Philip was hunted down and killed. But the damage had been done and, once started, the conflagration spread and developed into three years of intermittent warfare commonly known as King Philip's War. The Aboriginals were supported by the

French and, through the supply of arms and ammunition, were actively encouraged in executing hit-and-run raids on the English settlements. Ongoing Anglo-French hostilities, which finally petered out in the mid-eighteenth century, led to the English evacuating large tracts of land, particularly in central Maine.

In 1685 Charles II died and the crown of England passed to his brother James. The reign of James II was to last only four years and was dominated by religious disputes. Charles had converted to Catholicism on his deathbed, and James openly subscribed to the same religion. The Protestant majority in England became incensed by the overt actions of James to subvert English government by promoting his Catholic cronies to powerful positions in court. Revolution was in the air, with the great mass of populace transferring their allegiance to William, Prince of Orange, who was viewed as the staunchest defender of the Protestant faith in Europe. William landed in England on November 5, 1688, and marched on London with scarcely a shot being fired. James fled to France to seek asylum at the court of Louis XIV. Though there were many plottings to regain the crown for James, none was successful, and he died in 1701, living out his last years as a monk.

Prince William had been fighting the French since 1672 with little respite, and the continual conflict had drained his war chest. Nevertheless, despite the obvious lack of funds, he managed to assemble a massive fleet to invade England and drive his father-in-law, James II, off the throne. The fleet sailed from Holland in October 1688, the prince's frigate leading the van. It consisted of more than six hundred vessels, including fifty men-o'-war, and hundreds of transports laden with cavalry, artillery, and cannon. The force comprised more than forty thousand men. It must have presented a brave sight as the fleet sailed through the Straits of Dover in plain view of the English. The landing took place in Devon during the first week of November, and was met with great rejoicing by the general populace. Known as the "Glorious Revolution," the conquest of England was subsequently achieved with hardly a shot being fired, James fleeing to seek refuge in France.

The history books describe in detail the momentous events involved, but a question arises: where did William get the funds required to assemble such a mighty force when his coffers were empty? This aspect of the revolution appears to have been ignored by historians. Some monies were sent from England by those sympathetic to his cause, but they were hardly of the scale required. The answer is believed to lie with the treasure-seeking exploits of Sir William Phips, a mariner from New England who discovered the wreck of one of Spain's richest galleons ever to be lost at sea.

Soon after William's accession to the throne, England was drawn into the general conflict against France, with war being declared on May 8, 1689. The citizens of New England took up arms with great fervour. Port Royal had become a centre of French privateering, and much New England shipping had suffered as a consequence. On April 20, 1690, the frigate *Six Friends*, of forty-two guns, sailed out of Boston along with the *Porcupine*, the *Mary* and four other vessels, carrying a total attack force of 736 men.

Under the command of Sir William Phips, the flotilla sailed north towards the Bay of Fundy with the avowed intention of cleaning out, once and for all, the menace that Port Royal had become to English shipping. Meneval, governor of Acadia, who resided at Port Royal, could offer little defence and he surrendered on May 11. A considerable amount of booty is reported to have fallen into the hands of the New Englanders. It was ten days after sailing into Port Royal that the British sailed back to Boston in the belief that old scores had been finally settled.

A few months later Sir William Phips was standing off Quebec. The attack was abortive and repulsed vigorously by the defending French. Eventually Sir William fled, but not without severe loss. The survivors limped back to Boston in November, their ships heavily damaged.

The British may have conquered Port Royal a fourth time, but they had not completely eliminated French resistance. For half a dozen years or so, New England farms were terrorized by Aboriginals fomented by the French. The scalping and victimization of the English settlers by Aboriginals wearing crucifixes reached such proportions that retaliation and retribution were inevitable. Nemesis came in the form of Colonel Ben Church, of Plymouth. Here was a man who fought fire with fire, and to whom death was the inevitable fate of those defeated in arms. Accordingly he harried the coasts unceasingly and devastated French settlements wherever they could be found. All to no avail. One year later, in 1697, William III signed a treaty with the French at Ryswick, to conclude what is commonly known as the War of the League of Augsburg. For the fourth time Acadia was handed back to the French!

No sooner was the ink dry upon the treaty papers than Governor Villibon of Acadia put forth manifestos claiming land to the south that was clearly under British occupation. Unable to enforce these demands he engaged in skirmishes, and fighting continued in a desultory fashion until 1702 when, once again, war broke out in full force. Hostilities became inflamed and Colonel Church re-embarked for Acadia. The Bay of Fundy was the main centre of his depredations, but French resistance was strong. In 1707 some formidable arms were dispatched to Port Royal under the command of Colonel March. Two men-o'-war attacked Port Royal, but the action was repelled with no uncertainty, and March was forced to a humiliating retreat to Boston.

Three years later, on September 29, 1710, Colonel Nicholson commanded a large fleet of British and New England ships, complete with transports and men and again attacked Port Royal. The French defended for a week before surrendering. For the fifth time in one hundred years Port Royal had fallen. Samuel Vetch, a companion of Nicholson, had in his possession a royal warrant that appointed him governor of Port Royal in the event of British arms carrying the day. For seven years Vetch proved a tireless administrator of the struggling settlement. Finally, the Treaty of Utrecht in 1713 ceded Acadia to Great Britain and peace descended upon the mainland of Nova Scotia. Only

Île Royale (Cape Breton), Île St-Jean (Prince Edward Island) and the various settlements along the St. Lawrence River, including the fortress of Quebec, were retained by the French.

Port Royal may have fallen into British hands as a final act in the long, simmering antagonism that had wracked the region since the first shots were fired exactly one hundred years earlier, however, the drama was to last another forty-six years before Anglo-French hostilities were resolved at Quebec. During this period the Fortress of Louisbourg was developed into what was thought to be an impregnable fortress. It was not. It fell in 1745 to an undisciplined force from New England and three years later was returned to the French following the 1748 Treaty of Aix-la-Chapelle. The British accordingly selected Halifax and constructed their own fortress to match that of their foe.

As Fort Beausejour, at Chignecto, posed a threat to territory now under British control, Fort Lawrence (located at the site of the present-day Nova Scotia Tourist Centre) was established to counter French aggression. Fort Beausejour eventually fell to British arms in 1755, and a few years later James Wolfe sailed from Halifax to retake Louisbourg (1758), and later Quebec (1759).

This brief history of Nova Scotia is illustrative of the large number of times that official hegemony over the territory of Acadia changed in the short space of a century or more. The region was sparsely populated, with the majority of French settlements clinging to the better farmland skirting the Bay of Fundy. Settlement of the Atlantic coast was virtually non-existent in those years of the late seventeenth and early eighteenth centuries.

Despite the wavering fortunes of war that beset the region, Mahone Bay and its innermost islands must have presented an admirably secluded spot, despite the existence of La Have fifteen miles to the south. This small French outpost, founded in 1632, had over the years suffered many changes in fortune, and towards the end of the seventeenth century it probably consisted of no more than two dozen families striving to make a living from land and sea.

CHAPTER 9

An Ancient Mariner

I fear thee, ancient Mariner!
I fear thy skinny hand!
And thou art long, and lank and brown,
As is the ribbed sea-sand
   "The Rime of the Ancient Mariner" (Coleridge)

The name of Sir William Phips in connection with the Money Pit on Oak Island has received scant attention by other writers. This is somewhat surprising, for British archives contain thirty-five pages of carefully copied script on identical paper, with identical ink, accompanied by official testimonies to the fact that the two copy writers concerned were both official record clerks of the Government of Massachusetts. The papers relate to William Phips, his family and his neighbours on the Sheepscot River in Maine. The originals date from 1625 at the earliest to 1737 at the latest, the copies all being made in November 1750, more than fifty years after Phips's death in 1695. These copies were

Sir William Phips (1651-1695)
was knighted in 1687.

received in London the following February. Each transcript is innocuous by itself, but collectively the copies are meaningful, for the volume of correspondence in which this sheaf of papers can be found mostly relates to the 1753 settlement of Lunenburg, Nova Scotia. It is natural to query the relation between Phips and Lunenburg, but since the town lies only ten miles as the crow flies from Oak Island, the connection appears quite obvious.

Phips may be considered a local man, having been born and bred in Maine. He was well acquainted with the waters of New England and Acadia and twice made assaults upon French Canada. He had been successful in locating the wreck of one of Spain's most richly laden galleons, an exploit that had earned him his knighthood. He is, perhaps, one of the most colourful characters of his day, and is worthy of some serious consideration in relation to the Money Pit. For fuller details of his career, from backwoods to governor of the Massachusetts Bay Colony, reference should be made to the excellent biography by Emerson Baker and John Reid, *The New England Knight*.

William Phips was born on February 2, 1651, at what has been described by his friend, Cotton Mather, as "a despicable plantation on the river of Kennebec" in Maine. This description appears to be both exaggerated and unwarranted. His birthplace is, in actual fact, located in a delightful setting. It occupies a point of land, now known as Phipp's Point, which juts southwards into Hockomock Bay, between the estuaries of the Kennebec and Sheepscot Rivers. The coastline is indented with many creeks and backwaters, and there are numerous islands in the vicinity. It is interesting to note that one of the closest islands to the old Phips homestead is called Oak Island! The coincidence of names between Oak Island, Nova Scotia, and Oak Island, Maine, is considered nothing more than that — a coincidence, but a very curious one. Oak Island, Maine, was noted for its abundance of oaks and associated species, all valued for shipbuilding, and many small coastal vessels were built along the banks of the Sheepscot River. Undoubtedly young William was well acquainted with Oak Island and the oaks that grew thereon.

William Phips's father was an immigrant gunsmith from Bristol, England, although there is little evidence that he ever actively pursued his trade after landing in the New World in 1620. The hardships of winning a livelihood from the sea and forest, of clearing land for crops and pasture, of keeping body and soul together during the long, hard, inhospitable winters would have been a full-time occupation. And there were many children! William Phips was one of the youngest, reportedly being the twenty-first of twenty-six children. His father died while William was still young, and his mother remarried, which explains the vast brood of siblings. It was a hard life, and it is not difficult to imagine the privations the family suffered in their isolation.

At the age of eighteen young William left his backwoods home to seek his fortune in Boston, where he became apprenticed to a ship's carpenter. He did well and returned to the Sheepscot River to begin shipbuilding, at a location now believed to be in the vicinity of Phipp's Point. In the summer of 1676, Aboriginal attacks devastated the struggling settlements following the outbreak of King Philip's War. One girl is reported to have escaped a massacre, running twelve miles through woods and swimming a river in her flight, in order to warn the neighbouring inhabitants. William Phips's first vessel was in the process of completion, and his first act on hearing of the attacks was to embark the entire population of the area and carry them to safety. The region was virtually depopulated of European settlements well into the eighteenth century as a result of the war.

The picture of William Phips in those early days is of an ambitious, pushy, independent and spirited individual. He probably upset more than a few people, some of whom considered themselves well above him in that class-conscious society. He married a wealthy Boston widow and soon after went off to sea as captain of one of his own ships.

From Boston he traded along the New England coast, to Newfoundland and the West Indies, and is reported to have been in his early thirties when he began trading to the Bahamas. There he heard tales of the untold wealth that lay beneath the surface of the sea in the form of sunken Spanish treasure ships. No doubt his aspirations to both wealth and honour were fuelled by his exposure to this contagion.

The Bahama Banks had been the watery grave of many a Spanish plate ship on the homeward run from Vera Cruz and Havana, and the beachcombers of New Providence made a good living, if an erratic one, from wrecks in the general vicinity. It is known that in the early 1680s Phips worked a wreck there, though the pickings were reportedly modest. However, it was a useful apprenticeship, and other wrecks attracted his attention. With all the tavern-talk and bar-room gossip that Phips heard, there was one tale that fuelled his imagination above all others: it was that of a Spanish galleon that had been driven onto a reef some forty years earlier. It was reputed to be one of the largest vessels that had ever been lost and to be filled to the brim with gold, silver and jewels. Since the wreck had never been discovered it was a mouth-watering, if elusive, prospect. Phips set about finding it. Here was wealth beyond the dreams of Croesus!

On one of his returns to Boston, Phips decided to raise funds for this enterprise, having astutely concluded that his own resources were inadequate. The good people of Boston refused to venture their hard-earned savings to his hazardous proposition, possibly due to concerns about his reputation for being of a bellicose disposition. His quicksilver temperament and too-persuasive tongue were viewed with suspicion. He was perforce required to seek sponsorship elsewhere if he was to obtain the necessary funding to realise his dreams. Thus, with extraordinary audacity, he vowed to approach the man at the very pinnacle of British society — the king himself. Phips promptly gathered up all the money he could lay hands upon, packed his things for a trip of indeterminate length and took passage for England. It is not necessary to detail the frustrations that he faced before he managed to present himself to Charles II at the palace of Whitehall. The king proved receptive to persuasive pleading, and though four months earlier he had dispatched two vessels to the West Indies on a similar mission, the king was not averse to sending a third. Thus William Phips received his sponsorship.

The greatest feat of treasure-seeking, and one that is still admired throughout the world, is William Phips's location of the wreck of the

Spanish galleon, *Nuestra Señora de la pura y limpia Concepción*, commonly referred to as the *Concepción*. The ship had left Vera Cruz on July 23, 1641, arriving in Havana on August 27, from where she finally sailed on September 20, as the *almiranta* of the homeward-bound treasure fleet. The Spanish plate fleets always sailed in convoy with the largest vessel, known as the *capitano*, in the van and the second largest, known as the *almiranta*, in the rear. Though the *Concepción* was the largest vessel in the homeward bound fleet of 1641, she was relegated to *almiranta* because her seaworthiness was considered doubtful by the fleet commander, who sailed in the leading vessel.

August 20 was considered by the Spanish authorities as the very latest date for sailing from the Indies, in order to avoid the hurricanes and the inevitable bad storms that beset the Caribbean in the fall. Thus, the fleet sailing from Havana that year was one month late in departure. It was an ominous delay, though possibly unavoidable, as there had been no sailing of the treasure fleet back to Spain the previous year from Vera Cruz. Doubtless the King of Spain's coffers were in dire need of replenishment, and the colonial authorities felt better prepared to face the wrath of the Almighty than the wrath of their king!

The Spanish operated two treasure fleets in the Atlantic. The Neuva España fleet traded between Spain and Vera Cruz, bringing back the riches won from the mines of Central America; the Tierra Firma fleet traded between Spain and Cartagena. A Pacific fleet also operated out of the west coast of America, trading with the Far East. Porcelain, silks, spices, works of art and other valuable items were brought via the Philippines to Acapulco, hauled overland by mule train to Vera Cruz, and thence carried to Spain by the Neuva España fleet.

The *Concepción* was a somewhat larger galleon than most engaged in carrying treasure, being of 650 tons, 140 feet in length and 44 feet in beam. She was built in Havana in 1620 and boasted 36 bronze cannon. Her master and co-owner in 1641, Captain Eugenio Delgardo, was aboard on that last tragic voyage, a voyage that departed Havana carrying 496 souls, more than 300 of whom were to meet their doom. Since goods and chests of treasure are reported to have been stacked shoulder high in the ship's passageways, the ship must have been very heavily laden, perhaps dangerously so, with commensurate loss of freeboard. Her high poop deck, characteristic of such vessels, and her heavily laden state, are suggestive of difficult handling in running seas and stormy weather.

The *Concepción* was virtually doomed before she set sail out of Havana. Since arriving at Vera Cruz the previous year nothing had been done to the ship while she rode at anchor before the fort of San Juan de Ulloa. The tropical sun had melted the pitch in her joints, her rigging and cordage had rotted, and the voracious *teredo* (shipworm) had feasted upon her hull in those limpid waters. Don Villavicencio, the newly appointed captain of the *Concepción*, is reported as having been angry with the authorities, not only with regard to the seaworthiness of the ship and her relegation to the position of *almiranta*, but also in subordinating him to a pilot by the name of Bartholomé Guillen, who had never previously piloted a vessel on the hazardous homeward voyage. Guillen, from all accounts, appears to have been completely incompetent, and Villavicencio's worst misgivings were duly realized. Beset by storm since departing Havana the *Concepción* drove onto a coral reef forty-one days later on October 31, 1641, with great loss of life. The tragic story is told in a thrilling manner by Peter Earle in *The Treasure of the Concepción*.

Of all the plunder that the Spanish were to wring out of their possessions in the New World, fully one-third is estimated as having been contraband. Francisco Granillo, the chief boatswain's mate on the *Concepción*, later claimed that there was known to be on board more than four million pesos of treasure, not counting that belonging to His Majesty. If this is true, and there would seem no benefit for Granillo to lie, the total value of goods laden at Vera Cruz and Havana could far exceed other more conservative estimates of between four and six million pesos. In today's monetary terms these figures are somewhat meaningless because the market valuation on recovered artifacts is unlikely to have any relation to the raw bullion value, and would magnify it manyfold.

Sir John Narborough (1640-1688) Knighted 1673

William Phips, totally ignorant of the history of the sunken fortune that awaited him, but confident of its ultimate recovery, eventually sailed from England on September 5, 1683. Charles II had placed him in charge of the *Rose of Algeree*, the equivalent of a sixth-rater, equipped with eighteen guns and a complement of ninety-five men. The *Rose of Algeree* was quite a big ship for the time and was one of those captured by Sir John Narbrough off the coast of Morocco some years earlier. Phips must have been a very proud man now that he was in charge of one of the king's men-o'-war. The commission he had been granted by the king included the phrase:

> ...for the obtaining or gaining of all such plate, silver, bullion, gold and other riches as they or any of them can, in, by, from or out of any wreck or wrecks, lying or being amongst the said Bahama Islands or in any other place or places thereabouts in any of his said Majesty's, the King of England's, dominions.

Lord Christopher Monck (1653-1688), 2nd Duke of Albemarle.

The agreement with the crew was 'no purchase, no pay,' a phrase familiar to those with buccaneering experience. This first voyage lasted almost two years, and was quite unsuccessful in locating the remains of either the *Concepción* or any other vessel worth working for treasure. Nevertheless some silver was picked from a wreck off New Providence, and the *Rose of Algeree* did not return entirely empty-handed. The king's share of the spoils of the voyage amounted to a meagre £470 19s 8½d — not enough to cover the subsequent repairs to the ship.

Charles II had died before Phips's inauspicious return to England, the throne being assumed by his brother James. King James, however, was not going to be lured into any more speculative treasure-seeking ventures at the Crown's expense, and Phips was forced to seek less regal patronage in funding a second expedition, if there was to be one.

It is said that Phips was "tall, beyond the common set of men, and thick as well as tall, and strong as well as thick," a man who had quelled a mutiny by the sheer force of his personality. This sunburned giant of a man had a persuasive tongue in his head, and in less than a year he had found private backers. These included Lord Christopher Monck, the 2nd Duke of Albemarle, who had been removed from the service of James II, and Admiral Sir John Narbrough, Commissioner of the Navy. On September 12, 1686, two ships under the command of William Phips set sail from the South Coast of England — the *James and Mary*, of two hundred tons and twenty-three guns, named in honour of the king and queen, and the sloop *Henry of London*, of forty tons.

Several of the former crew of the *Rose of Algeree* found their way on board these two vessels. A significant difference for the crews on this second voyage to the Bahamas was that they were to receive wages. The 'no purchase, no pay' condition of service was abandoned. This condition had been the cause of much dissent among the crew of the *Rose* and had led to mutiny on the previous voyage.

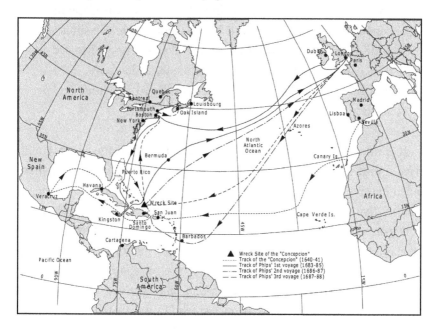

Figure 32
Map of the North Atlantic and the Voyages of Sir William Phips

It is unnecessary to dwell upon the subterfuges that Phips had to undertake to avoid the unwelcome interest of the Spanish authorities in Hispaniola. He traded for a few weeks in the goods he had brought with him, accepting in return such commodities as tobacco, cowhides, meat and rice. Then on January 12, 1687, he dispatched the *Henry* to "make search for ye wreck." On January 20, having had only two days on the reef, divers located the wreck about which they had all dreamed since leaving England. The logbook of the *James and Mary* records dramatically the reception of the *Henry* when the good news was reported:

> This day (7 February) towards 4 a clock Mr. Rogers (of the 'Henry') came in who gave us to understand that they had been on ye banck and told us they had don as much as any men could doe.... This morning (8 February) our Captain sent our long boat on board Mr. Rogers which in a shoart time returned with what made our hearts very glad to see which was 4 shows, 1 bar, 1 champene, 2 dowboys, 2000 and odd dollars by which wee undeerstood that they had found ye wreck.

It is interesting to speculate why Captain Rogers of the *Henry* could have found the wreck of the *Concepción* so quickly after so many had failed before, including Phips himself. The explanation appears to lie in the fact that this time Phips had taken the trouble of seeking out survivors from the tragic events of 1641, who had settled on the north coast of Hispaniola. From them he had gleaned the information that, after being wrecked, the rafts they had constructed took a southwesterly course before striking land. Previously everyone had assumed this course to have been southerly. Thus the area to which Phips dispatched the *Henry*, in order to commence the search, was actually some sixty miles east of where he had sought the fabled wreck on the former expedition.

Between February and April 1687, a vast fortune, mainly in silver, was recovered. Without the assistance of two additional ships, a sloop and a shallop belonging to William Davis of Bermuda and Abraham Adderley of Jamaica, the recovery would not have been so great. On some days more than a ton of silver was recovered. One logbook entry reads:

> Our boats went to work on ye wreck and in ye evening brought on board 2,399 pounds weight of coynd silver which we suppose were in chests which wee putt in 32 baggs.

The *James and Mary* returned to England carrying a cargo of silver amounting to 68,512 pounds troy weight, slightly in excess of twenty-eight short tons. The estimated value was £205,536 (about £3 million in today's currency), and the cost of the voyage amounted to a mere £3,200. This was a truly enormous return on investment, of staggering proportions for even the most avaricious speculator in any century!

In view of the abundance of wealth in silver that Phips had stumbled upon, it is certain that his overwhelming priority was to remove as much as possible before his operations were interrupted. Predatory corsairs and privateers of rival nations would have shown little respect for him or his crew. Later expeditions were to disclose that the *Concepción* had broken apart on the reef, and the detached stern lay some 150 yards off from the midship and bow sections from which Phips recovered large amounts of silver. His divers were few in number, and relied purely on the ability to hold their breath under water in order to retrieve the treasure and bring it to surface from a depth of forty-five feet. It is doubtful, therefore, that on this first visit to the wreck site he was aware of the detached stern, which would have yielded a far greater wealth of booty. Having already possessed himself of a proverbial king's ransom, and bearing in mind his vulnerability from interlopers, who can blame him for his prudence in hauling up anchor and making speed for England with the intention of returning in force and better equipped at a later date? On June 6, 1687, the *James and Mary* anchored off the South Coast of England, and before long the country was abuzz with the news of William Phips and his success.

It would only be human nature for the Spanish to attempt to lay claim to the treasure that they had lost forty-six years earlier. Their protestations, diplomatic and otherwise, needless to say were repulsed by the British. What the British had won from the deep by their skills, ingenuity and luck, was to remain in their hands. On June 28, 1687, William Phips was knighted by James II for his service to the Crown. A commemorative medal was struck, with the heads of James II and his consort on the obverse, and the *James and Mary* with two boat crews fishing for treasure on the reverse. The humble lad from that poverty-stricken village in the backwoods of Maine had risen like a comet in genteel society and could now rub shoulders with British nobility.

There is an interesting story told about Phips's meeting with the king. On receipt of his knighthood Phips was requested by James to name "anything he wanted" as an additional reward for his services to the Crown. Phips is reported to have requested the return of the charter to the New England colonies that had recently been revoked by the king. James apparently laughed when Phips made his request and retorted "anything but that." To a man of integrity and proud of his colonial background, the incident is likely to have rankled, and possibly festered. It may have been the thin end of the proverbial wedge that was to come between Phips and the king. Everyone knew that a contender lay in wait across the English Channel. William, Prince of Orange, son-in-law to James, and currently at war with Louis of France, was casting an acquisitive eye on the throne of England for his own political ends.

Sir William Phips, newly knighted, settled for the appointment of provost-marshal of New England. Only the governorship of Massachusetts was a higher appointment in the fledgling colony, a position eventually attained by Phips under the rule of William III. How such news of the increased good fortunes of Phips, the 'upstart from Boston,' must have been received by friend and foe alike back home! Many a self-opinionated 'noble' must have felt remorse in not having treated him a little better in earlier days.

It took little time to organise another expedition back to the Bahamas, where the *Concepción* lay wrecked upon the Silver Bank, so-called because of the hoard of silver that it had yielded. With a surplus of funds available, the original stakeholders needed no additional backers, though there was one newcomer, Thomas Neale, Master of the Mint. The new flotilla included the *James and Mary*; the *Henry*; the king's frigate *Foresight*, of 520 tons, under Sir John Narbrough; the *Princess* under Francis Rogers, who had previously captained the *Henry*; the *Good Luck*, a our-hundred-ton merchantman commanded by Sir William Phips; and the Duke of Albemarle's yacht, the *Boy* (or more properly the *Boy Huzzar*) under the captaincy of Thomas Monck, the Duke's nephew. Accounts suggest that Phips appeared to have exhibited some reluctance to return to the scene of his exploits. The flotilla sailed on September 3, 1687, three months after the triumphal return of the previous expedition.

It was December 15, 1687, when the *Foresight* arrived on the Silver Bank and the captain reported that the wreck site was swarming with ships. They had come from all over the West Indies, and the English colonies of North America. Those that already had a good haul of treasure on board were quick to take off.

The presence of one of His Majesty's warships on the scene, intent on establishing an official British presence, by force of arms if necessary, was not to be reckoned with lightly. How much treasure had been removed by these reported 'interlopers' will never he known. Sir John Narbrough's estimate is given to be as much as £250,000, somewhat greater than Phips had recovered on his second, most fruitful voyage, though Sir John's estimate may have been on the high side for reasons that will become clear. This still left at least £500,000 of booty aboard the wreck, if the Spanish ambassador to England could be believed. However, official bills of lading of Spanish treasure were notoriously understated, as the previously mentioned testimony of Francisco Granillo, who sailed as chief boatswain's mate on the *Concepción*, implies.

The Capitano of the Spanish treasure fleet in which the *Concepción* sailed in 1641, the *San Pedro y San Pablo*, managed eventually to limp across the Atlantic after the fleet had been scattered by the same storms that drove the *Concepción* onto the reefs of the Silver Bank. The *San Pedro y San Pablo* ran aground in Spain whilst negotiating the sand bars in the estuary to the Guadalquivir River. Recovery operations may have been easier than those for her sister ship stranded on an ocean-bound reef in the Bahamas, but the official reaction was acutely embarrassing for all concerned. The *San Pedro y San Pablo* was found to be carrying huge amounts of gold, silver and precious jewels not recorded on the manifest documents. Thus it may be concluded that the wreck of the *Concepción* still held a vast quantity of booty, despite the inroads that had been made by Phips on his earlier voyage, and other looters in the interim.

First laden at Vera Cruz, the *Concepción* subsequently took on extra cargo at Havana, before departing on that fatal voyage. The total cargo is reported to have comprised, "apart from silver, a large quantity of gold in bars and worked objects, 43 chests of pearls, 21 chests of emeralds from Columbia's Muzo Mine and 436 chests of trade goods from the Far East, including a large quantity of Chinese porcelain." This constituted an enormous sum of wealth, especially bearing in mind that Phips, on his celebrated first attempt, recovered only silver.

The five ships of the English fleet had a total complement of almost four hundred men, half of whom were divers. Despite all this available labour, no more than 275 pounds of silver was reportedly recovered on the best day (February 17, 1688). The official explanation for this low haul, which contrasted greatly with that of Phips on the earlier expedition, was that all recovery operations were concentrated on the midship and bow sections and that the aft section of the ship was totally overgrown by hard coral. The *Concepción* had in actual fact parted on striking the reef, with the stern drifting away towards the south. Beneath the high poop deck, enclosing the luxurious staterooms of the nobility, would have been the plate-rooms with their hoards of gold bullion and precious jewels, and the private, undeclared riches of the favoured. The various bags of coined silver, the sows, bars, champenes, dowboys of silver, and pieces-of-eight already recovered from the wreck site would have been paltry in comparison to that in the stern section, which lay still unrecovered. It would be expected that as the *Concepción* drove headlong onto the reef, thereby holing her bow and beginning to take on water, the stern would have risen. More vulnerable to the wind because of her high poop deck, great stress would have been imposed on the hull in the vicinity of the mainmast. When the ship split and the stern section separated, a trail of ballast and wreckage would have been left on the seabed linking the two detached sections of the wreck.

This second expedition, better equipped and with more divers, would have found the trail of ballast and wreckage leading to the stern section 150 yards distant. Three hundred years later ballast stones from the *Concepción*, with bottles attributed to Phips' expeditions, were still to be found on the seabed by latter-day treasure-seekers. Once the stern section was found there was much booty for the picking! The official explanation of hard coral preventing access to the aft section of the *Concepción* is highly suspicious, as young coral is relatively soft.

Sir William Phips, on the *Good Luck*, hauled up anchor on May 8, 1688, with the stated intention of departing for Boston, there to take up without further delay his position as provost-marshal of New England. Phips had spent five months at the wreck site. Sir John Narbrough never did return to England. He died three weeks later, on May 27, 1688, as the result of a fever raging through the fleet. On August 2, officers of the Crown came aboard the newly returned *Foresight* in the River Thames to receive the treasure brought back to England. It weighed only 3,213 lbs 10 ozs, a vast difference from the twenty-eight tons that Sir William had hauled out of the ocean deeps the previous year.

Other attempts were made to work the wreck site, that of William Robinson perhaps being the most noteworthy. This expedition, with three ships, set off in late 1688, but was to return as empty-handed as that of Sir John Narbrough. The sponsors of the several expeditions that followed hard on the heels of Phips's successful treasure-hunting spree of 1686–87 were equally the poorer as a consequence. From that date, the *Concepción* was left to mind her dead in a watery grave.

More recently the wreck site was rediscovered, with some fortunes falling to those adventurers that searched for it using modern technology. Some artifacts, jewels, china and tarnished pieces-of-eight have been recovered, notably by Burt Webber and Tracy Bowden. The *National Geographic* of July 1996 contains photos of the dazzling jewelry and Ming Dynasty china recovered by Webber and Bowden. However, no significant quantity of treasure has ever been recovered by these later expeditions. The vast treasure in bullion, plate, jewels and precious porcelain known to have been carried within the holds of the *Concepción* appears to have disappeared into thin air. Or has it?

Sir William Phips returned New England on June 1, 1688, after an absence of almost five years. It is rather puzzling that he should prefer to bring his ship *Good Luck* into Portsmouth, New Hampshire, rather than into Boston. Portsmouth was outside the jurisdiction of Governor Andros in Boston. Though an able and honest man, Andros had made himself very unpopular with the colonists by his zeal in executing the king's instructions, which included, among others, the breaking down of powers held by certain ruling Puritan groups, and revocation of their charters. Phips and Andros were at odds with one another right from the start.

Though Phips had been absent from home for many years, apart from the return to Boston for a few weeks in the fall of 1683 while in command of the *Rose of Algeree* en route to the Bahamas, it was a mere six weeks or so before he set sail once again. The records tell us that, due to various slights and difficulties placed before him by Andros, he felt himself incapable of carrying out the duties that had been vested in him by virtue of his position. It is reported that an attack was made upon his life. Phips set off for England reportedly to seek redress from the king, and it was to be the best part of a year before he returned. Where did he go? The records are vague. Certainly he was in England part of the time, where momentous events occurred. William of Orange landed at Torbay, Devon, on November 5, 1688, and King James II fled to France on December 24; but Sir William Phips appears to have played no major role, or any role worth mentioning, in these stirring events. He might just as well not have been in England at all. It is known, however, that he was certainly there in late August and September 1688, before the revolution, and then again between mid-January and mid-March 1689, during which time he had contact with Lord Mordaunt, a confidant of William, Prince of Orange. Lord Mordaunt had visited the wreck site of the *Concepción* in February 1688 with five Dutch men-o'-war, under strange circumstances. He had remained in the Caribbean for three months, leaving the same day as Phips.

When Phips did eventually return to Boston on May 29, 1689, it was to find that his fellow citizens had risen up against Andros seven weeks earlier and locked him in jail. An unknown Boston writer of the period states:

> As soon as Intelligence arrived concerning his present Majesty (ye Prince of Orange) his Heroic understanding to deliver ye English nation from Popery & Slavery This Androsse Emitted or caused to bee printed at Boston January 8, 1688 a proclamation against ye Invasion from Holland as Hee there calls it charging Every person in New England Especially all officers Civill & military that They should to their utmost oppose ye blessed design of ye Prince. These things & many other the like did so Exasperate ye People as that They rose as one man & Abdicated Andresso & his Evill Instruments from ye Government.

On his return Phips assumed command of the frigate *Six Friends*, with a complement of up to 120 men. For the better part of the following year he cruised the coasts of New England and Nova Scotia ostensibly seeking out, raiding and destroying pirate strongholds. We are not told where he went on this roving commission, or what success he encountered.

In April 1690 the New Englanders decided to take the initiative in the war France had declared as a result of the revolution in England the previous year. The General Court of Massachusetts appointed Phips to lead an expedition against Port Royal and to impress up to five hundred men for such service, with the results described in Chapter 8.

A few months later, in October 1690, Sir William Phips, in the *Six Friends*, was standing off Quebec, leading an attacking force of thirty-one ships and 2300 men, which had departed Boston two months earlier. The attack was repulsed vigorously by the defending French, causing great loss amongst the English, and the survivors limped home to Boston with their tails between their legs. It has therefore been concluded that the attack was abortive. But was the attack as abortive as it seems? There is a fascinating aspect to this incident directly relevant to Oak Island and its lost treasure.

The tactics adopted by Phips in his 1690 attack on Quebec have been analysed many times by military analysts. They generally reach the consensus that the attack was made too late in the season, that a promise of arms and ammunition from England did not arrive in time and that progress up the St. Lawrence River was hampered by contrary winds and lack of pilotage. Nevertheless, Phips and his men expended a great deal of effort in pillaging the French settlements of Percé, Mingan, Anticosti and Tadoussac as they ponderously made their way upriver to Quebec. Military commonsense suggests that *if* the capture of Quebec was the prime object of the expedition, then the fleet would have made its way upriver as swiftly, silently and as stealthily as possible, harnessing all resources of manpower, ammunition and supplies, and refraining from alerting the French to its presence for as long as possible, contrary winds or no. Instead the tactics adopted by the English resulted in the fleet becoming depleted of ammunition, the crews riddled with disease, a general shortage of rations, and the enemy scurrying to reinforce Quebec to repel the perceived invasion. The lateness of the season alone in mounting this abortive attack suggests an ill-considered act on the part of Phips, as the season was neither propitious for a lengthy siege nor a successful outcome. But Phips was no rash or foolish man. He may have been overbold, and often impatient at times, but never rash or foolish.

By the time Phips had anchored off Quebec, his men, weakened and ravaged by disease, were in no condition to mount a vigorous assault. Even if the English had managed by some stroke of fortune to take the city, they could never have held it through the approaching winter. Temporarily its capture may have boosted morale, but a realistic appraisal of the military supply logistics involved suggests that this fledgling force would never have held the city for any length of time. These considerations imply the existence of an ulterior motive for the attack, a motive yet to be recognised by historians and military analysts, and one that also may not have been known to those hardy volunteers who left home and hearth in New England to participate in this inglorious feat of arms. The only long-lasting effect resulting from the disastrous assault was that French forces were withdrawn from the Acadian peninsula, and for a few years that particular region of New France never became a battlefield in any attempt by the French to regain lost territory. If this was the overriding strategy for the invasion, then the assault on Quebec may be considered to have been a complete and total success. For the next seven years the British could come and go as they pleased, with little fear of military confrontation.

An unknown writer participating in the onslaught upon Quebec describes part of the engagement in which Sir William was personally involved in the following terms:

> Sir William Phips with His men of warr came Close up to ye Citty. He did acquit himself with ye greatest bravery. I have diligently enquired of those that know it who affirm there was nothing wanting on his Part Either as to Conduct or Courage. Hee ventured within Pistoll shott of their canon, & Soon beat them from thence, & battered ye Town very much. He was for Some hours warmly Entertained with their great Guns. The vessel wherein Sir William Commanded had 200 men. It was shot thro' in an hundred places with shot of 24 pound weight; yet thro' ye wonderfull providence of God, but one man was killed & two mortally wounded in that Hott engagement, which continued ye greatest part of ye night and ye next day several hours.

In February 1691 Sir William embarked for England to plead support for a second attack upon Quebec. He was absent for over a year,
returning in the *Nonsuch* on May 14, 1692. By this time he had been
appointed governor of the Massachusetts Bay Colony, an appointment
that was confirmed by William III on January 3, 1692.

Sir William is reported to have governed Massachusetts in a rough-
shod manner, perhaps suitable for the pioneering settlement it was at
that time. The *Dictionary of American Biography* states this about him:

> In commercial matters he stood for the old free-trade policy,
> thwarted the customs officials at every turn, connived at
> piracy, and neglected to preserve the king's share in con-
> demnations... Socially Sir William seems always to have been
> at a disadvantage. A "self-made" man, he made a display of
> fraternizing with ship carpenters and former friends of lowly
> station, a trait as irritating to the aristocracy as his pompous
> manner or the undignified outbursts of temper with which
> he met opposition to his will. At times he could not resist
> resorting to brute force. He publicly caned a captain of the
> royal navy who refused to obey his orders, and on another
> occasion dragged the collector of customs around the wharf
> for attempting to seize a vessel suspected of illegal trading.

In the fall of 1694 Sir William was summoned to London to answer
various charges brought against him by his numerous enemies. On
February 28, 1695, he died from a sudden ailment (probably influenza)
and was buried in the church of St. Mary Woolnoth in Lombard Street,
London, a church later destroyed by bombing in World War II.

CHAPTER 10

The Mordaunt Conspiracy

While you here do snoring lie
Open-eyed Conspiracy
His time doth take

Ariel in "The Tempest" (Shakespeare)

Charles Mordaunt (1658–1735) was one of those eccentric individuals who, from time to time, flit across the stage of British history, fascinating us with their antics, but mystifying us even more as to why they act as they do. Ten pages in the *Dictionary of National Biography* are devoted to Mordaunt, but precious little relates to the first thirty years of his life, the years before the Glorious Revolution of 1688. Before this event Mordaunt achieved nothing to any purpose, and nothing with any lasting effect. But after William, Prince of Orange, was offered the crown of England on February 13, 1689, he was heaped with honours. These honours included appointments as privy councillor (February 14), gentleman of the bedchamber

Lord Charles Mordaunt (1685-1735) 3rd Earl of Peterborough

(March 1), colonel of a regiment of foot (April 1), first lord of the treasury (April 8), Earl of Monmouth (April 9), lord lieutenant of Northamptonshire (April 29), colonel of horse (June 15) and water-bailiff of the Severn (August 9). King William obviously did not lose much time in rewarding Mordaunt for whatever he had done for the cause of revolution, and this has perplexed historians. One biographer wrote of him:

> ...when not engaged in more honourable or adequate employment, he was perpetually mixed up in conspiracy and intrigue. His conduct could neither be foreseen nor trusted. He was as dangerous to his friends as to his foes.

Mordaunt's appointment to the post of First Lord of the Treasury is particularly curious, especially as he was one of the most improvident individuals of the age, unable to keep his own financial affairs in order, let alone those of the nation. Macaulay, in his *History of England*, writes about him in the following terms:

> Mordaunt, one of the most vehement of the Whigs, was placed at the head of the Treasury; why, it is difficult to say. His romantic courage, his flighty wit, his eccentric invention, his love of desperate risks and startling effects, were not qualities likely to be of much use to him in financial calculations and negotiations.

Mordaunt's passion for conspiracy and intrigue was one of his greatest assets. He had been forced to flee England shortly after the accession of King James in 1685, for he had spoken out boldly against the king's politics. By this rash act he placed his life in jeopardy, and he sought refuge at the court of the Prince of Orange in Holland, where he devoted himself to the cause of revolution, continually beseeching William to invade England and oust James from his throne. His was not a lone voice crying in the wilderness: seven prominent men, one of whom was a bishop, were in the vanguard of growing public dissent. This group became the nucleus around which the strategy of revolution revolved. Mordaunt, ever eager for intrigue, made numerous clandestine visits to England to help foment a groundswell of public strife and disorder, a necessary prelude to revolution. Even with a price on his head and the king's officers on the lookout for him at every seaport Mordaunt managed to evade capture. In later years Mordaunt was active in political intrigue throughout Europe and turned up like the proverbial 'bad penny' on almost every battlefield of the age.

The previous chapter made reference to the visit by Mordaunt to the wreck site of the *Concepción* in February 1688, a visit that lasted three months, during which Phips and Narbrough were engaged in diving for treasure. It is noteworthy that when Phips eventually left the wreck on May 8 in his *Good Luck*, with the avowed intent of sailing alone to North America, Mordaunt and his men-o'-war sailed the same day. This is too coincidental. An unarmed merchantman like the *Good Luck* was always vulnerable on the high seas to pirates and privateers, more so if her holds were filled with treasure. Mordaunt and his Dutch men-o'-war can thus be perceived as necessary to provide vital protection, not only to the wreck site while treasure was being hauled from the deep, but to escort Phips's treasure-laden vessel wherever it was bound. The purpose of Mordaunt's visit to the wreck may have puzzled historians, but his wily temperament and his prolonged stay of three months, before sailing the same day as Phips in the *Good Luck*, is highly suggestive of the existence of a conspiracy of which he was the ringleader.

Conspiracy is an ugly word. The dictionary definition is "to unite together, usually for an evil purpose — to plot." Depending on the gravity of the conspiracy lies the penalty, if the conspiracy is revealed. By the prevailing norms of the seventeenth and eighteenth centuries, execution would be warranted if the conspiracy were proven treasonous. Plotting to defraud the king of vast amounts of treasure would certainly fall within this category. But then one might be tempted to ask — which king? The object of the 'Mordaunt Conspiracy,' as it will be termed, was to win the treasure from the *Concepción* and place it at the disposal of William, Prince of Orange, in order to help finance the invasion of England. Could any conspiracy be driven by higher motives, or the conspirators be more selfless in the interests of the nation? Mordaunt's meteoric rise in the affairs of state suddenly becomes explicable when he is viewed as the genius who managed to bring massive amounts of wealth within the grasp of the Prince of Orange.

All revolutions need financing, and one involving a full-scale sea-borne invasion of England needed plenty of money. The Prince of Orange had been at war with France for a quarter of a century: his war chest was empty, his coffers depleted. Money was needed to pay soldiers and sailors, to hire ships and to purchase weapons, powder, ammunition, uniforms, rations for men, fodder for horses and the seemingly infinite array of stores and supplies required to support an army on the move. An acquisitive eye was turned upon the booty that could be recovered from the wreck site, booty useful in paying the inevitable bills. Mordaunt, with his zest for political intrigue and his eye for opportunity, must have envisaged a vital role for Phips after the treasure-laden *James and Mary* arrived home in June 1687.

It is not surprising that William Phips was reported as being reluctant to return to the wreck site that same year, for King James had created him a knight to reward him for his triumph, the first colonial ever to be awarded such honours. The conspiracy being touted by Mordaunt must have borne heavily on Phips's conscience, and it must have seemed a treasonous act.

There is some hint that Mordaunt returned to Holland in the summer of 1688, taking with him some of the treasure, probably some or all of that portion that could be easily rendered into specie to pay the invasion troops. This would have been a prudent move on his part, for it vividly demonstrated the tangible nature of the riches about to fill the coffers of the king, following a successful outcome to the revolution. The 'Mordaunt Conspiracy' must have seemed a godsend to the needy Prince of Orange. But by July 1689, Mordaunt had fallen out of favour, presumably the new king having become aware of his deficiencies, or had learned of the loss of the Money Pit and the immense treasures contained therein, which likely comprised the bulkier treasures recovered from the *Concepción*.

The major stakeholder in the treasure-seeking venture was Lord Christopher Monck, 2nd Duke of Albemarle (1653–88), the son of the famous General Monck who had played an important part in the civil wars of 1641–52 and a vital role in the restoration of the monarchy. The younger Albemarle was a great favourite of King Charles II, but after Charles's death in 1685 he fell out of favour with the new king, James II. This loss of favour resulted in the Duke being deprived of all his high positions in the affairs of state. The rupture seems to have had its origin in a violent quarrel that took place between the two men in private on July 30, 1685. It is useless to conjecture what was actually said in the passion of the moment, or on what subject, but James is reputed to have harangued Albemarle at great length. The following day the Duke handed in his various commissions, and resigned all public appointments.

The Duke of Albemarle had an old ally in Jamaica, one by the name of Sir Henry Morgan. After his buccaneering days were over Morgan had twice got himself into trouble, which had led to his being transported to England in chains on both occasions (1674 and 1681). Instead of being placed on trial, Morgan was freed as a result of the Duke's intercessions with King Charles. He returned to Jamaica, his standing and reputation undiminished. The Monck family had held widespread interests in the Caribbean for many years, but in 1686 the Duke of Albemarle requested, and was awarded, the position of Governor of Jamaica. The date of this appointment tallies with the period when Phips was seeking sponsorship for his second voyage, after the first voyage in the *Rose of Algeree* had proved such a dismal failure.

The Duke appears to have decided to make his abode in Jamaica shortly after the triumphant return of William Phips in the treasure-laden *James and Mary*. During the summer of 1687, while feverish preparations were being made for the return expedition to the wreck, equally feverish preparations were being made in the Duke's household to move himself, his possessions and his entire household to Jamaica. Whether there was any intention on his part to subsequently return to the more temperate climes of England will never be known, but his assumption of the post of Governor of Jamaica and his de facto control of English affairs in the Caribbean gave him widespread powers. From his vantage point in Jamaica he was in a prime position to manipulate British naval movements and maintain the wreck site free from any prying eyes more loyal to the king during the recovery operations of 1687–88. In this connection it is interesting to observe that all the naval officers involved in the expedition, no matter how minor their involvement, received promotions in rank after the Prince of Orange assumed the Crown of England. Albemarle was to die before the year 1688 came to a close and the seeds of revolution had begun to bear fruit. He died in Jamaica on October 16, two weeks before the invasion, apparently jaundiced either as a consequence of disease or from his habitual drinking.

The second major stakeholder in Phips's treasure-seeking expeditions was Sir John Narbrough (1640–88). He would have held a pivotal role in any conspiracy being advanced by Mordaunt, for they were old shipmates, having served together in the Mediterranean during the Anglo-Moor wars. Narbrough was of humble parentage and had risen, through his own unaided efforts, from cabin boy to admiral. He had seen much action and suffered wounds that dogged him to his dying day. By inclination he was a puritan devoted to his country. Though holding a great admiration for James when he had been a commander of the fleet in the days of King Charles II, it is doubtful whether he would have allowed this friendship to prejudice his patriotism. Narbrough died at the wreck site on May 26, 1688, succumbing to a fever that swept through the fleet. This sad event took place a couple of weeks after Phips, in his *Good Luck*, had departed for North America, his hasty departure spurred by the fever beginning to rage through the fleet. Narbrough's body was buried at sea.

It is significant to the link between the treasure of the *Concepción* and Oak Island that in May 1695 there was an official inquiry into the estate left by Albemarle. The complainants included the Viscountess Falkland, wife of the deceased Lord Falkland, one of the original stakeholders in the treasure-seeking expeditions, and other surviving participants. One of the questions asked of the witnesses brought forward was the following:

> Do you know of any gold, silver, treasure or other riches taken up by the order or on the account of the Duke of Albemarle whilst he was Governor of Jamaica? If you do, to what value and how and to whom was the same or any part disposed or applied? Have you any book or books kept concerning the same and by whom and in whose custody did you see such book or books and when and where and what is the sum of the same and in whose possession?

The witnesses called knew nothing of any gold, silver or treasure that might have remained unaccounted for. Or if they did they weren't talking! The fact that the enquiry was initiated by the minority stakeholders suggests that they might not have been convinced that all the treasure won from the wreck of the *Concepción* was accounted for.

Lord Mordaunt, the Duke of Albemarle, Sir John Narbrough and the newly knighted Sir William Phips must be viewed as the most important conspirators in the plan to ensure that the bulk of the riches won from the *Concepión* was passed on to William, Prince of Orange. Others were undoubtedly involved, including senior members of the ships' crews. The motives of Mordaunt, Albemarle and Narbrough were likely, in the main, honourable, though Albemarle's is likely to have been more self-serving than the others. That of Phips is difficult to judge. The success of the expedition of 1686–87 had given him a reputation and earned him a knighthood. It is likely that he was somewhat apprehensive about throwing in his lot with other conspirators. A sense of disloyalty to the monarch, James, could have weighed heavily upon his conscience, thereby explaining his seeming reluctance to return to the wreck site on that final expedition. As we have seen, however, he did go. As the man who knew most about recovering treasure from the site, and who knew of numerous secluded spots along the war-wracked coasts of North America where the treasure could be safely cached until after the revolution, Phips was indispensable to the group.

The conspirators would have been well aware of the detailed scrutiny to which the records of the 1687–88 expedition would be subject on return to England. At the end of every voyage all ships' journals and logbooks had to be forwarded to the Secretary of the Admiralty for inspection. This practice had been initiated in 1686 by the ever-vigilant Samuel Pepys, who was determined to root out corrupt and erring captains in his pursuit of an efficient navy. It is not surprising, therefore, that the various logbooks and journals from the 1687–88 expedition to the wreck site reflect an exceptional degree of conformity in the descriptions of the difficulties the expedition encountered. In particular, the inability to break through the coral supposedly encasing the stern of the *Concepción* is consistently related in the logbooks. It is now known that although coral does grow fast it does not grow either fast enough or hard enough to completely entomb a wreck within forty years or so. In fact young coral is relatively soft. Thus the official records must be disputed on this point alone, bringing the veracity of the whole into question. The records describe large numbers of vessels looting the wreck when the *Foresight* first arrived. There is no way of independently verifying this. The implication is that the records were written to fool both Samuel Pepys and the king, to whom Pepys was intensely loyal. Whether Pepys and the king had any suspicions that the official reports were deliberately falsified is not known. If they had such suspicions they might well have been forgotten in the rising tide of revolution.

The movements of Sir William Phips in the year or so following his return to Boston from the wreck site are of great interest. He left ostensibly for England on July 16, 1688, and is reported to have arrived at the Downs on August 17, but on what ship is not known. This would have allowed him sufficient time to first take his ship *Good Luck*, with the *Boy Huzzar* in attendance, to Oak Island and to leave his loyal crew with instructions to commence the shaft of the Money Pit. With his Dutch allies in attendance there would have been no difficulty with an ongoing voyage. In view of the considerable volume of treasure on board, the *Good Luck* would have remained at Oak Island. When he might have returned again to Oak Island we do not know, but he did not reappear in England until early January 1689. This period of more than three months, between September 26 when he was last sighted in England and his reappearance on January 10, would have been adequate to complete the excavation of the Money Pit shaft and to consign any treasure on board the *Good Luck* to the imagined safety of its depths. Following his return to Boston on May 29, 1689, six months after the revolution had taken place, he was probably confident that all he need do was to set sail and recover the treasure. He is reported to have boasted, "I have no need at all to look after any further advantages for myself in this world; I may sit at home if I will, and enjoy my ease for the rest of my life."

Phips immediately took control of the frigate *Six Friends* to patrol the coasts. It may be conjectured that during this period he attempted to recover the treasure he had so laboriously cached a few months earlier. The result was calamitous, as we have concluded. Since the treasure could not be regained easily or quickly, it was desirable to occupy the territory to facilitate more involved and lengthier recovery attempts. This may explain why Phips was in the forefront of advocating attacks on Canada and prepared to lead the charge on those two occasions in 1690.

CHAPTER 11
Military Involvement

Let fame, that all hunt after in their lives,
Live register'd upon our brazen tombs
The King in "Love's Labour's Lost" (Shakespeare)

A priceless treasure had been lost upon a desolate island on the far side of the wide Atlantic, and none could tell the reason. William Phips and his co-conspirators could not recover the treasure which had been consigned to the depths of the Money Pit. What was to be done? No time would have been lost in mounting another recovery expedition, but when that and successive attempts failed, then what? Eventually, the government would have been forced to conclude they had no alternative but to flood the workings to prevent the treasure falling into the hands of others. This would ensure it was buried for eternity, and no one would know it was there. Or so they thought!

One can be certain that a curtain of secrecy would have shrouded any work on the island. The immense worth of the lost treasure would have made sure of that, for its value is estimated at about $60 million in today's terms (see Chapter 12), or £3 million in the 1690s, a sum equivalent to twice the annual tax revenue of the British government. Only competent engineers, aided by skilled miners, would have been entrusted with such work. This meant the military, as only they possessed the necessary skills and resources.

This chapter summarizes the evidence for a military connection to Oak Island. What follows is a reconstruction of how the Flood Tunnel was excavated and the Smith's Cove cofferdam constructed. Based upon new evidence we have accumulated, we are confident that what we present here is both rational and logical, helping to further unlock the mystery of Oak Island.

Any attempts to recover the treasure between 1690 and 1697, after which the territory was returned to France by the Treaty of Ryswick, were doomed to fail. The odds were stacked against success, for geological knowledge at the time was scant or non-existent, and the reason for the phenomenon that had led to the loss of the treasure in the first place must have confounded the finest military engineers of the age. These attempts would have left the remnant shafts and tunnels in the vicinity of the Money Pit, referred to in Chapter 7.

There is one intriguing piece of evidence to suggest that King William had a hand in these attempts since he formed a special corps of engineers, answerable only to himself. King William's Corps of Engineers, as it became known, was officially constituted in January 1696, and paid by direct warrant. Four years later it was formally disbanded. Regrettably, there is a total lack of archival information relating to the clandestine activities of this elite group, which has confounded historians. The suspicion must be that the corps was involved in attempts to recover the treasure prior to the territory being returned to France in 1697.

For the following half century, Britain was embroiled in so many conflicts and so many military engagements that the government likely neglected the Money Pit on Oak Island and the dazzling wealth it contained. Neglected it may have been, but not forgotten.

The entire mainland of Acadia lay largely ignored by London, even though the territory had been ceded to Britain by the Treaty of Utrecht in 1713. A smattering of administrators attempted to govern a fractious and hostile population composed largely of Acadian settlers and Aboriginals. During this long period Nova Scotia was governed from Port Royal (now Annapolis Royal), but the settlement was too far removed to counter the military threat posed by the bastion of Louisbourg in the French colony of Ile Royale, and that of Fort Beausejour strategically located on the isthmus of Chignecto. The extensive harbour of Chebucto, now Halifax, promised to provide both military security to thwart French attacks, and a more central location for administration of the new colony.

Edward Cornwallis (1713–76) was appointed governor, charged with the colony's foundation, and arrived in Halifax in June 1749 to take up his governorship. For the next three years he devoted his energies to establishing the settlement, fending off attacks, and commencing construction of its defences.

Cornwallis was succeeded by Peregrine Hopson in 1752. One of Hopson's biggest headaches was the dispersal of new immigrants. Several locations outside the new metropolis were considered. One was Musquodoboit, another was Merliqueche (now Lunenburg). He chose the latter. Hopson may have acted with the best of intentions but, nevertheless appears to have been censured. There is no record of the correspondence he received from their lordships in London, but his replies to them are extant, and couched in language that is blatantly apologetic or, worse still, grovelling. He eventually resigned in November 1753 on grounds of 'poor eyesight,' yet this did not prevent him from participating in British attacks on the French West Indies in 1759. The man who replaced Hopson as governor was Charles Lawrence. Unlike Hopson, an unwanted child who had been placed in the army at eight years of age, Lawrence was a highly connected relative of the Earl of Halifax. Lawrence had arrived in the colony in 1747.

Evidence, which follows, points to the conclusion that the scheme to construct the Flood Tunnel was executed in the period immediately following the assumption of Charles Lawrence to the position of governor of the colony, that is in the period 1752–54. It was during this period that the settlement of Lunenburg commenced, with the first settlers arriving in June 1753. Reference has already been made in Chapter 1 to the clauses inserted into land grants signed by Colonel Lawrence mentioning 'mines of gold and silver, precious stones and lapis lazuli,' in other words 'treasure.' It is obvious, therefore, that he must have been privy to the scheme. Also, his personal supervision of the establishment of the settlers gave him a valid excuse to remain in the area while work on the island was in progress.

One characteristic of the Flood Tunnel that reflects its military origins is its internal dimensions of 2½ feet wide by four feet high, as mentioned in Chapter 3. In 1824 the Royal Engineers Establishment issued *Rules for the Practice of Military Mining in any Soil excepting Rock*. A relevant section reads:

> The smallest branch *[tunnel]* in which a man can work conveniently, is 2½ ft wide in the clear, by 3 ft high. Any excavation about 3 feet wide and more than 4 feet high, obtains the name of a gallery, 3 feet by 4½ feet is one of the smallest…To prevent mines excavated in loose soil from falling in, the earth is usually retained by woodwork, consisting of rectangular frames, placed at intervals of about 4 feet apart, and of short planks extending from frame to frame. The latter composes what is technically called the 'sheeting.'

Convinced that the military were involved in the construction of the Flood Tunnel, we decided to look for evidence of who exactly was responsible. Our search led us to the library of the Corps of Royal Engineers at Chatham, Kent. Lists of military engineers employed by the army were available, though the records were incomplete, since the Corps of Royal Engineers, as presently constituted, did not exist prior to 1772. Before this date, groups of sappers and miners were organized on a company basis, each company generally consisting of two sergeants, two corporals and thirty-odd men under the command of one or two officers. The army employed many skilled craftsmen, each appointed to a regiment as its 'engineer.' The engineer was often responsible for a wide range of activities: construction of camps and blockhouses, fortifications in the form of earthworks and palisades, storage of ordnance and explosives, maintenance of cannon and heavy artillery, as well as sapping and mining when besieging or being besieged.

An invaluable source reference in our search proved to be *History of the Corps of Royal Sappers and Miners* (1855), in two volumes, by T.W.J. Connolly (1815–85), who was a soldier and clerk at the Woolwich and Chatham engineers' establishments. He researched the history of the corps and produced the volumes at his own expense. Unfortunately, Connolly only dealt with the history of the corps from about 1757, after its members were awarded military rank. His detailed notes supporting the published volumes, held by the Library of the Royal Engineers at Chatham, occupy seventeen hand-written foolscap notebooks. A second valuable source was *History of the Corps of Royal Engineers* (1889) in eleven volumes. Volume One (1889) written by Major-General Whitworth Porter, provided names connected to the Nova Scotia establishment immediately prior to official formation of the corps in 1772.

These source documents provided the link for which we were searching. One entry in Connolly's notes was of particular interest, for it makes reference to a certain William Bontein, who was born into a coal-mining family at Killearn, Stirlingshire, Scotland in 1726, and whose elder brother, Archibald, was also an engineer in the British Army. The entry is a note instructing Bontein to proceed to:

> ...Annapolis via Camborne dismissed from June 1, 1752 and thence 4/- [shillings] a day more out of money for works under order of June 12, 1752.

What this note means, in modern parlance, is that Bontein was to be taken out of active service and dispatched first to the tin-mining centre of Camborne in Cornwall, and then to Annapolis, and to be paid an extra four shillings per day out of money budgeted for a specific project. His normal rate of pay was five shillings per day. This 80 per cent pay raise to nine shillings per day therefore represented a substantial wage increase! A raise of this sort was not customary for overseas assignments and indicates the importance of the 'works' he was about to undertake.

Bontein's tunnelling exploits during the war in Flanders (the War of the Austrian Succession, 1744–48) would have brought his name into prominence among his superiors as a competent and trustworthy tunneller. The order of June 12, 1752, suggests the purpose of his visit to Camborne was to recruit or pick up a group of previously selected miners. It also raises the question of ongoing transportation to Annapolis.

Based on extant newspaper reports, the ninety-ton *Gale*, master Thomas Casson, was an immigrant ship, which departed Rotterdam on June 5, 1752, cleared formalities at Gosport (Portsmouth) on June 13, and arrived at Falmouth, the nearest port to Camborne a distance of some fifteen miles, on June 28. This was an unusual port of call for an immigrant ship, as such vessels were not known to visit Falmouth. The sixteen-day period between receiving his orders in London and the arrival of the *Gale* at Falmouth would have been sufficient for Bontein to travel to Cornwall and prepare men and equipment for the ongoing voyage. The *Gale* sailed four days later on July 2, 1752, bound for Halifax, Nova Scotia, where it arrived on September 15. The voyage took 110 days, longer than usual, and there were twenty-nine deaths during the passage.

Immigrant ships were far from commodious. The ship owner made his money by transporting as many souls as could be crammed aboard, and space was always at a premium. Settlers were allocated space according to sex and age, and records indicate that no room was left unoccupied on previous or subsequent sailings of the *Gale*. However, for the 1752 sailing, John Dick (the European agent for the British Government) grumbles in a letter found in the National Archives at Kew, and dated December 22, that twenty bed-places were vacant when the *Gale* left Rotterdam that year. There is no record of who took passage at Falmouth, but we think it is reasonable to assume that William Bontein and his Cornish miners occupied the vacant space to which Dick refers. This space likely included room for mining tools and specialist equipment and from this we deduce that some twelve to fourteen miners accompanied Bontein to Nova Scotia.

Further support for the conclusion that Bontein's miners were recruited from Cornwall comes from the presence of several artifacts recovered from the Money Pit in the 1930s, after excavation of the shaft was extended to previously unrecorded depths. One of these was a poll-pick, the significance of which has been discussed in detail in Chapter 5, as it was of a type favoured by Cornish tin miners.

A year earlier Governor Cornwallis had written, "Annapolis is of no consequence compared to Halifax," and militarily speaking he was correct. Why, then, was Bontein, with his tunnelling expertise and skilled miners, directed to Annapolis, whose days were numbered, instead of Halifax? The answer seems to be that there was another engineer, older and senior to Bontein, at Annapolis. His name was William Cowley, and he held the post of Chief Engineer for Nova Scotia. Cowley was a stonemason by profession, but had previously gained much experience in constructing wharves and maritime defence works in the Mediterranean. He had been sent to Annapolis in 1743.

Though Bontein and Cowley were skilled military engineers in their respective fields of tunnelling and maritime works, neither had much seniority in the Corps of Sappers and Miners as then organized. In fact neither held military rank, and their status was quite lowly, for they could not initiate projects of any great duration or cost. There was only one engineer in Britain who would have held the respect of government, been privy to its confidences, and possessed the necessary authority to initiate measures to construct the Flood Tunnel as we understand it today, and to whom Bontein and Cowley were directly answerable. That man was Colonel Thomas Lascelles, Chief Engineer of Great Britain, who had held the post since 1742.

Thomas Lascelles, however, died in November 1751 at the age of eighty-one, and all authority in North America for the initiation and execution of engineering works devolved upon Captain John Henry Bastide (c.1698–1770), Chief Engineer for North America. We can therefore attribute the concept of the Flood Tunnel, to ensure flooding of the Money Pit in perpetuity, to either or both of these men, though the actual execution of the project would have come under the direct charge of Bastide.

Though engineers such as Bastide, Bontein and Cowley would have been vital to the success of any military engineering project, a large support group of labour would also have been necessary, much along the lines of an army pioneer corps today. The British Army only employed professional miners in its tunnelling activities, for it was perceived as a specialist occupation. However, a large labour force was always necessary to hoist and stockpile spoil, cut timbers for supports and so on. Under Cowley's direction this labour force would have constructed the protective cofferdam for the tunnel intake works, excavated and removed soil from the filter beds, placed selected drainage materials and on completion dismantled and hidden all evidence of the operations. A number of trades was likely involved, especially carpenters and blacksmiths.

In our search for a likely candidate for this support group we came across another curious piece of evidence concerning the strength and movements of military units at that time — in particular those of the 47th Regiment of Foot.

In 1750, two years before Bontein sailed from Falmouth, the 47th Foot, under the command of Colonel Peregrine Lascelles (1684/85–1772), a cousin of Thomas Lascelles, was ordered to Nova Scotia from the regiment's base in Ireland. Another family member, William Lascelles (born 1694/95), had arrived in Nova Scotia a year prior to the arrival of the 47th Foot. It is likely he also was involved in the proposed engineering works on Oak Island, acting as deputy to his cousin, Colonel Peregrine Lascelles. The 47th had arrived in Nova Scotia in August 1750. Its strength is listed as ten companies of men totaling 340 privates and non-commissioned officers (including ten drummers), with thirty-five officers, including surgeons and a chaplain. In addition the 47th brought with it from Ireland 209 women, children, and servants. In total the regiment consisted of almost sx hundred people. Its first act after disembarkation at Halifax was to march to Minas, thence to take ship to Beaubassin, where six months earlier an abortive attempt had been made to establish a British foothold in the disputed isthmus of Chignecto.

Military historians admit there is an absence of information concerning the activities of the 47th while in Canada, at least up to the attack on Louisbourg in 1758. A War Office letter dated April 11, 1755 indicates that the regiment's strength had become seriously depleted since its arrival in Halifax. It read:

> His Majesty having been pleased to order each of the regiments of foot commanded by Major-General Warburton [45th] and Colonel Hopson [40th] to be augmented with 10 sergeants, 10 corporals and 300 private men, and Major-General Lascelles Regiment of Foot [47th] with 20 sergeants, 20 corporals, 10 drummers and 710 private men.

The proposed increase in numbers of the 47th, in order to bring the regiment up to fighting strength for the future attack on Louisbourg, is virtually double that for either of the other two regiments. Why was the 47th singled out for such a massive increase in comparison to other regiments? When the 47th took the field at Louisbourg the strength of the regiment is listed as comprising nine hundred men plus officers, making a total complement of 949. However, when the 47th arrived from Ireland its total strength is listed as only 375, of which 340 were privates and non-commissioned officers. With the proposed addition of "20 sergeants, 20 corporals, 10 drummers and 710 private men," as indicated by the above quoted War Office letter, the total (excluding officers) would have risen to eleven hundred. But only nine hundred men took the field.

Two hundred men from the ranks had gone 'missing.' Not all of them would have died, been transferred or deserted. Where did they go? Military records regarding the attack on Louisbourg make reference to Bastide, who was responsible for the reduction of the fortress, being accompanied by "eleven engineers, as many miners, and 90 carpenters." No doubt the miners were those who had accompanied Bontein from Cornwall, but excluding these, Bastide's engineering force comprised another hundred men. From where did they originate? The most likely explanation is that they had served under him on Oak Island previously. Drawn from the ranks of the 47th Bastide would have selected those who had shown the greatest aptitude as blacksmiths, carpenters, masons, and associated trades. By virtue of their clandestine activities on Oak Island, this group of some two hundred strength were not part of the 47th and thus were not included in the count of nine hundred men in the 47th when they took the field in Louisbourg. After the battle, these men were employed by Bastide for demolition at Louisbourg, and then for construction at Halifax.

Captain Bastide must be viewed as the most important, though not necessarily the most senior, British Army officer involved in the Oak Island project. The project would have been, after all, an engineering venture of great importance to the government, and Bastide was the foremost military engineer in British North America. However, because of its secrecy, overall military control of non-engineering matters would have rested in the hands of a man such as the somewhat elusive William Lascelles, deputy of Colonel Peregrine Lascelles, if not in the hands of the colonel himself. In this connection it is interesting to note that Peregrine Lascelles was promoted to the rank of Major-General on March 27, 1754, a point at which a successful conclusion to the project might have been anticipated.

We can summarize our suggested military hierarchy as follows, using project management terminology in vogue today:

Design Concept Engineer: Colonel Thomas Lascelles (succeeded by Captain John Bastide).
Project Manager: Colonel Peregrine Lascelles; deputy William Lascelles.
Project Engineer: Captain John Henry Bastide.

Section Engineer (Tunnels): Mr. William Bontein.
Section Engineer (Cofferdam): Mr. William Cowley.

Bearing in mind the secret nature of the enterprise, and the necessity to minimize the wagging of tongues, the only secure place for those engaged upon the Oak Island workings would have been on Oak Island itself — but where? Certainly not in close proximity to the works. The obvious place for a construction camp to house the workforce was towards the west end of the island. It will be recalled that an old track, running east-west across the island, was noted by early treasure-seekers. Such a track could have represented the daily 'commute' for the hundred-plus workforce engaged on the project at the height of operations.

From the evidence of shaft excavation that was found on South Shore, it appears that the engineers initially considered the best route for the Flood Tunnel would follow the shortest distance from the Money Pit to the sea. A connection to South Shore is a distance of about 320 feet. Any proposed tunnel would have involved excavation along this line in an attempt to establish such a link, and this would have required some form of cofferdam at the seaward end. No remains of a cofferdam has been discovered at South Shore, as far as is known. However, there is evidence that attempts were made to excavate such a tunnel, or at least an access shaft in order to commence tunnelling towards the Money Pit. As described in Chapter 6, geologist Robert Dunfield dug a trench along South Shore in 1965 and encountered an old shaft that could not be ascribed to any previous searcher or group engaged on seeking treasure. The circular shaft was eight feet in diameter, and when opened up by mechanical excavator was shown to be at least fifty-four feet deep.

The following year Dan Blankenship deepened the shaft to ninety feet. He found evidence that the diggers had encountered difficulties in attempting to overcome caving ground, a problem he himself also encountered, for he could go no deeper. Layers of clayey soil, decomposed peat, and boulders indicated they had been deliberately placed.

This evidence suggests the purpose of the shaft was to attain sufficient depth to commence tunnelling from South Shore towards the Money Pit on an upslope grade. Virtually without exception, tunnellers prefer to excavate upslope. This permits the face to drain freely of any water they may encounter, and for spoil to be removed more readily. Therefore, any design concept would have incorporated a tunnel in which the face was advanced progressively upslope.

An overall gradient of five percent would mean that the shaft would have to be dug to a depth of about 110 feet to intersect the Money Pit shaft at a depth of about 115 feet (see Figure 33). But the miners experienced difficulties with unstable ground, either due to large inflows of water or quicksand. Consequently, attempts were made to stabilize the bottom of the shaft by backfilling with the materials discovered by Blankenship and shown in Figure 33. An adequate supply of boulders from the beach close to hand and peat from the nearby swamp easily accounts for the five feet of boulders and eight feet of peat in the shaft. The overlying layers of red sandy soil and blue clay represent a further attempt to provide a permanent top seal.

We believe that the difficult ground conditions encountered by the miners were sufficiently problematic to require a rethink of the original concept. With the shaft eventually stabilized at a somewhat higher level (a depth of sixty-five feet), considerable debate must have ensued on whether to proceed with the original plan to tunnel from South Shore to the Money Pit, or to abandon the plan entirely because of the perils involved. If the seal placed at the bottom of the shaft proved defective, then miners could be trapped and entombed within any heading being driven towards the Money Pit. Perhaps the difficulties in the shaft had already taken their toll. In addition, it would have been apparent that tunnelling from the sixty-five-foot depth would have resulted in a rather high intersection with the Money Pit shaft.

Often it has been suggested that the Money Pit is linked to South Shore by a second flood tunnel, though there is no valid evidence

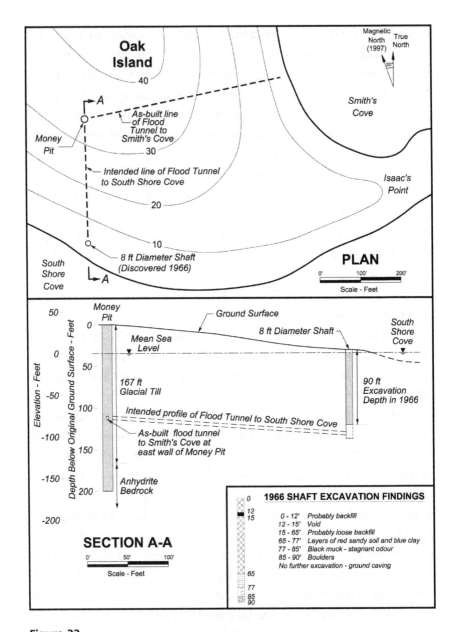

Figure 33

Findings in South Shore Shaft in 1966 and Alignment of Intended Flood Tunnel

of one. The water-soluble nature of the bedrock, and the hazardous ground conditions encountered in the first attempt by the military to make such a link, suggest otherwise. However, it is certain that hydraulic connections do exist between the Money Pit and South Shore through solution channels within the anhydrite, and these are the consequence of prolonged pumping in the search for treasure.

Whatever their reasoning, it is clear that the engineers must have abandoned their original tunnel and conceived an entirely new one. As we now know, the Flood Tunnel, as finally constructed, links the Money Pit with Smith's Cove, a significantly longer distance of five hundred feet.

The Flood Tunnel has not been fully explored, but as mentioned earlier is generally considered to be 2½ feet wide by four feet high. We would expect, however, that enlargements were made at intervals along its length for storage of tools and equipment, to facilitate the passage of men, materials and the removal of spoil arising from the excavation process. A rough estimate indicates that a minimum of about four hundred tons of soil were removed, under dangerous conditions that at best can be described as arduous and cramped. Like human moles, the miners toiled away deep underground, their only illumination the light from a flickering candle or oil lamp.

In view of the potentially disastrous ground conditions encountered excavating the access shaft on South Shore, we presume that a similar shaft was excavated to an appropriate depth at Smith's Cove, though no such shaft has ever been found. If tunnelling was to commence from the Money Pit to Smith's Cove it was essential that good ground prevail through the entire length of the proposed tunnel. No sane miner would tunnel towards the sea without putting his mind at ease on that score! To what extent tunnelling proceeded from both ends simultaneously must remain a moot point. The section of tunnel excavated from the Money Pit end was undoubtedly the greater, but to reduce the toil and increase the overall rate of tunnelling it must be presumed that some excavation was commenced from Smith's Cove.

It was reported by the Halifax Company in 1867 that the intersection of the Flood Tunnel with the Money Pit showed the tunnel to
have an upward gradient of 22½ degrees, or 40 per cent. Such a gradient could not be maintained the length of the tunnel without breaking
through to the surface, thus it may be assumed that a lesser overall
gradient prevails, probably between five and ten degrees, or 9 to 12 per
cent, and this suggests that the grade varies along the tunnel's length.

Excavation of the Flood Tunnel would have employed procedures
in practice at the time. In anything other than hard rock, frames are
installed at regular intervals of four to six feet to ensure stability. These
are known as 'setting frames' which often incorporate mortise-and-
tenon connections at the corners. This enables the frames to be wedged
into position to maintain line and level by 'chocks' (also known as
'chogs' or 'cogs'). These carefully positioned frames permit boards,
known as 'spiles,' to be driven ahead of the excavation to provide
overhead protection to miners at the face. Any side protection would
involve the use of 'close sheeting' or 'open sheeting' depending on the
likely potential for collapse of the tunnel walls. Good, sound glacial till
would only require the use of occasional sheeting. Figure 34 illustrates
the approach likely used to advance a tunnel in the manner described
above.

We know that the Flood Tunnel was backfilled with beach stones,
probably along its entire length. The stone backfilling served two main
functions: first, to prevent tunnel collapse; and second, to facilitate
rapid recharge. Stones for backfilling would have been relatively large
and uniform to ensure high rates of water flow — the inclusion of too
many small stones would diminish that rate.

The removal of several hundred tons of tunnel spoil during excavation, and its replacement with a similar volume of beach stones, would
likely have been facilitated through the tunnel by a hand-operated
winch, pulleys and an 'endless rope.' During backfilling it is unlikely
any tunnel support timbers would have been removed, though floor
planks would have been taken up to supply air to the workers at

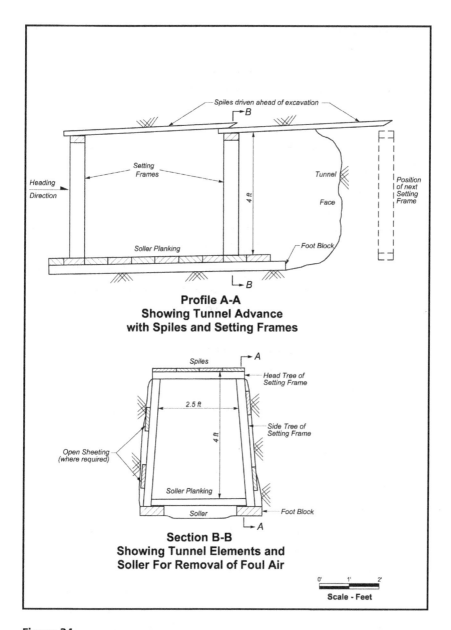

Profile A-A
Showing Tunnel Advance
with Spiles and Setting Frames

Section B-B
Showing Tunnel Elements and
Soller For Removal of Foul Air

Figure 34

Typical Approach to Advance the Flood Tunnel Using Setting Frames,
Spiles and Sheeting

the retreating face. Any timbering remaining in the tunnel could be expected to rot.

The excavation of a tunnel access shaft at Smith's Cove would have required the construction of a small protective cofferdam. Later this would have been incorporated into a larger structure to enable construction of the filter drains and intake system. Doubtless, part of the larger cofferdam would have included a section for berthing craft and unloading supplies.

The remains of a cofferdam structure (and filter drains) were discovered at Smith's Cove in 1970, and have been fully described in Chapter 6. The cofferdam included inclined hewn timbers (six by seven inches), attached to a line of embedded horizontal logs (twelve to twenty inches in diameter) by two-inch oak dowels at four-feet centres, each attachment location being denoted by carved Roman numerals in sequence. Wide planks of two-inch thick hardwood were secured to the base of the inclined timbers, the method of fixing not being reported. Sawn boards, or cross-members (nine feet long by 6½ inches wide by five inches deep), rested transversely upon the horizontal log at intervals of eight to nine feet. These carried shallow notches three feet apart. There was no evidence that the cross-members were fixed by dowels or nails, and it must be presumed they were originally lashed to their supports, the lashings subsequently having rotted.

How would these remnant timbers, fragmentary as they are, be incorporated into a completed cofferdam? We advance the following reconstruction:

The remnants suggest that its engineers used a technique similar to the one used in the construction of a number of eighteenth- and nineteenth-century forts in British North America, some of them erected to resist U.S. territorial expansion following the War of Independence. One of these, Fort Ingall, at Cabano, Quebec, was built in 1839 to garrison two hundred men, and has been reconstructed in recent years. Figure 35 is a photograph of the model on display at Fort Ingall depicting the way the stockade wall, or palisade, was constructed.

Accompanying the model is the following description:

> Fort Ingall's largest defence work the stockade, was made of
> massive timbers interspersed with apertures through which
> arms could be fired. Archaeological digs led to the discovery
> of the wall's original outline and the techniques employed
> to build it. The stockade consisted of ten- to fifteen-foot
> tree trunks. To begin with a beam was buried horizontally
> 4 feet underground. Then with the help of diagonal beams,
> the main stake was anchored. Between each main stake
> there was a series of eight trunks, held by two cross-pieces,
> which formed a wall that protected the fort against attack.

This method of stockade wall construction must be considered
a military standard, and indicates how the Smith's Cove cofferdam
could have been built. Accordingly, Figure 36 depicts a conceptual
section of the complete cofferdam, incorporating the remains of the
timber structure revealed by the 1970 excavations. The earth cofferdam constructed at that time was lost through overtopping before the
excavations at Smith's Cove were complete, so it is likely that other
buried timbers exist of which we have no knowledge, but which were
associated with the original work.

The first stage in constructing the cofferdam would have been to
install the kingpost foundation beams (1) within the intertidal zone at
as low a level as possible. Each foundation beam, a massive baulk of
timber, would have been provided with a precut slot to accommodate
the base of a kingpost (2). At the same time, the longitudinal thrust
beam (3) would have been positioned outside the intended line of the
cofferdam wall on its seaward side. Such a beam placed longitudinally
would have provided what in soil mechanics terms is now known as
'passive resistance,' to resist the outward thrust of the stockpiled soil
behind the timber wall.

The second stage would have been to position and fix the inclined

Figure 35
Model of Palisade Wall at Fort Ingall, Cabano, Quebec

struts (4) at the same time as the kingposts were raised, and it is likely that the upper connection was made before raising took place. Trennels (wooden dowels, also known as treenails) were used at the lower connection with the longitudinal thrust beam and would also likely have been used at the upper connection with the kingpost. To ensure that the kingposts were vertical, any adjustment could be made by installing the lower trennels after the kingpost had been positioned. Since the inclined struts are likely to have varied in length from one

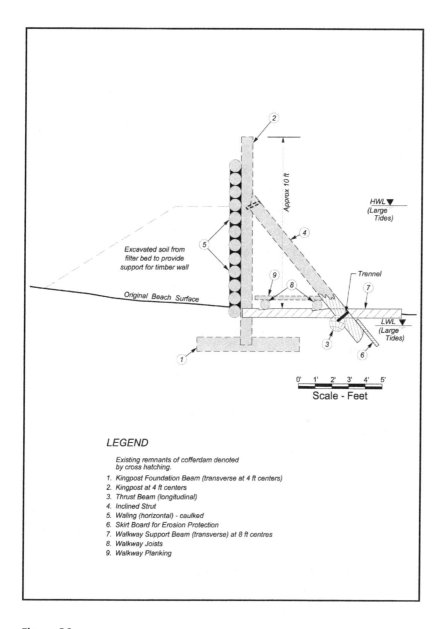

Figure 36

Inferred Design Section of Smith's Cove Cofferdam Merged to Existing
Remnants of Cofferdam

kingpost to another, they may well have been marked with a chisel — crude Roman numerals would have sufficed.

The third stage would have been to place the horizontal timbers (5), often referred to as walers, behind the kingposts and to caulk the gaps using oakum or coconut fibre. These wall timbers may have been lashed to the kingposts or fixed with trennels. Additional support would have been provided by the excavated soil as it was brought up from excavation for the filter drains.

To limit scour from tidal backwash, which might undermine the structure, a protective skirt (6) would have been provided in the form of a wide board securely fixed to the bottom of the inclined struts, its lower edge buried as deep as possible.

Finally, to ensure the cofferdam wall was watertight, it would have been necessary to provide access to the outside of the wall at low tide for inspection and recaulking. The final stage of cofferdam construction was, therefore, to place the cross-members (7), the joists (8) and walkway planking (9).

During the 1970 excavations a number of artifacts were found, mostly nails or spikes in various stages of decomposition. Among them, however, was a 'hand-forged wrought iron caulking tool.' This would have been an essential implement for those responsible for ensuring the seaward side of the cofferdam wall was maintained in good condition, undamaged by frequent storms during the construction period — a term estimated as between eighteen months and two years. It is a testimony to the skill of those military engineers that their cofferdam lasted longer than any constructed by later treasure seekers.

What is our proposed timeline for construction of the Flood Tunnel and its associated works? Some preparatory work would have taken place prior to the arrival of William Bontein and his group of miners in October 1752. Certainly, we must assume that all materials essential for the men to commence work, and which were provided from local sources, would have been ready to hand. A berth to offload supplies may have been required, and that the obvious location for such a berth would have been Smith's Cove, which is masked from the view of passing vessels by Isaac's Point (see Figure 33). It is likely much timber was brought to the island, in preference to cutting it on the island itself, in order to minimize the 'footprint' left behind on completion of the project. The belief is that much timber for this purpose may have been brought from Lunenburg as some clearing was reported prior to the arrival of the settlers, and doubt exists as to who was responsible.

Excavation of the first (abandoned) shaft on South Shore would have taken no more than about six to eight weeks. If the miners experienced troubles in overcoming caving ground — especially if a fatality occurred — the work may have extended to about three months. Thus by mid-January 1753 debate must have centred on the wisdom of proceeding with the proposed tunnel from South Shore to the Money Pit or choosing a second safer option, linking the Money Pit to Smith's Cove. For this second option to be proved feasible, the ground conditions had to be checked out to a satisfactory depth at the Smith's Cove end. If they proved consistent with those in the Money Pit, it might be presumed that tunnelling would be in the same type of soil for the estimated five hundred feet of excavation. A shaft, therefore, is likely to have been dug at Smith's Cove, which could be incorporated into the overall design. A few weeks is all that would have been required to confirm satisfactory ground conditions. This brings the project up to the end of February, or early March 1753.

Full-scale excavation of the Flood Tunnel likely commenced from the Money Pit in the spring of 1753 and took about eighteen months to complete. Progress was limited because no more than two men could have worked at the tunnel face at any one time, and it must be supposed the miners worked two- to three-hour shifts, twenty-four hours per day, except Sundays. Assuming three miners in each gang (two at the face and one at the portal in the Money Pit) Bontein would have had four to five gangs, which he could rotate on an orderly basis.

Hand excavation in the hard, tough, bouldery till would have been time-consuming in those dark, cramped confines. It is unlikely that excavation would have progressed any more than two to three feet per day at most, and possibly less on some days. Taking a likely average of two feet of progress per day, and 450–500 feet of tunnel to be excavated (about 200–250 cubic yards in volume), the excavation period is close to forty weeks. Following completion, the tunnel was to be packed with selected beach stones. This would likely double the time to (say) eighty weeks from commencement, or a total period of approximately eighteen months. If Bontein had commenced the Flood Tunnel in the Spring of 1753, it would have been completed by the fall of 1754. We know that by then Bontein was at Annapolis Royal.

With reference to establishing tunnel alignment and grade control, it is interesting to note the first surveying in the area was reported in 1753 in connection with the foundation of Lunenburg. This was performed by Charles Morris, aided by James Monck, who was later to play a role in the administration of the colony. James Monck was the grandson of an illegitimate brother of Christopher Monck, 2nd Duke of Albemarle, who had been pivotal in sponsoring Phips's voyage of discovery for the wreck of the *Concepción*. The fact that James Monck was on the island is interesting in itself, but more pertinent is the fact that the survey work was carried out in 1753. The word 'survey' is generally associated with establishing property boundaries and suchlike. However, construction surveying is equally important, if not more important when excavating a tunnel! If Charles Morris and James Monck were present on the island in connection with tunnel construction, it is likely to have been in the spring or early summer of 1753, immediately prior to the arrival of the settlers at Lunenburg.

Once excavation of the Flood Tunnel had commenced, with no hazards perceived that might hinder the project, cofferdam construction would have begun, followed by excavation and placement of drains and filter layers. All these activities, requiring a large labour force, would have been carried out at the same time as the tunnelling. The construction of these ancillary works would have dwarfed the tunnelling work but, unlike tunnel excavation, there was no constriction of space. We presume, therefore, that the entire project was largely complete by October or November 1754, though site cleanup to remove traces of human activity may have continued into 1755.

Demolition of surface structures would have included living quarters, stores, sheds and associated structures, the overall object being to leave behind as little evidence as possible of any activity on the island. Bearing in mind the hundred odd people involved in the project, accompanied by wives and family, demolition and cleanup could well have been a lengthy business.

The cofferdam would have been dismantled also. However, many deeply buried timbers would have been left in place, considering the excessive effort required to remove them from the water-logged soil in which they were embedded. Removal of the kingposts would have been an easy task once the inclined struts had been severed as close as possible to their connections with the longitudinal thrust beams. This is exactly what has been discovered at Smith's Cove thus far.

The site cleanup must have been carried out meticulously, and with great diligence, as few artifacts have been discovered that point to an extended period of military occupation. We regard this attention to detail as bearing further testimony to the importance the British Government placed upon conducting the operations in the utmost secrecy.

Our reconstruction may be considered somewhat speculative, but it is based on a familiarity with military engineering of the period, and our own experiences in underground excavations. There is much evidence to support it in the form of available British records, and archaeological findings on site. We believe more supporting evidence will be uncovered as exploration continues on the island. Also, archival evidence may well be found that corroborates — or conflicts — with our reconstructions. In the meantime our conclusion is that only the British government had the motive, the means, and the opportunity to excavate the Flood Tunnel and its appurtenant works on Oak Island. From an engineering standpoint this was a greater challenge than digging the original Money Pit.

CHAPTER 12

The Value of the Treasure

And the parrot would say with great rapidity,
'Pieces of eight! Pieces of eight! Pieces of eight!'
        "Treasure Island" (Stevenson)

If the prospects for recovering the treasure lost within the Money Pit are to be assessed, especially as regards the ratio of cost to benefit and profit, an assessment of its likely value is essential, regardless of the nature of the treasure. Any estimate, however, is fraught with uncertainty and conjecture.

Peter Earle in his excellent book *The Treasure of the Concepción* writes as follows regarding Spanish plate vessels:

> Single ships carried up to two hundred tons of silver. How much was there [on the *Concepción*]?...According to the Royal Officers at Vera Cruz the King's treasure sent in the fleet commanded by Juan de Campos totalled just under two and a half million pesos, representing royal revenue for two and sometimes three years from Mexico, Guatemala and Campeche, together with four registered chests containing gold, silver, precious jewels, pearls and gold dust... The King's silver was distributed half-and-half between just two ships, the *Concepción* and the *San Pedro y San Pablo*...A letter with full information on the weight of every bar and piece of silver was delivered to the silver-master (*maestre de plata*) of each ship...On the basis of this document one would assume that there was more than a million pesos of

the King's silver on each of the two ships...since the actual register has been lost, it is impossible to be sure what the true figure was.

It is even harder to estimate how much silver [and other valuables] was loaded on the *Concepción* by private individuals. Pedro de Medina [the *maestre de plata* of the *Concepción*] said that there was 500,000 pesos, but this seems quite absurdly small. Private remittances were nearly always much greater than royal remittances, and, since there had been no fleet home to Spain in 1640, one would expect the return [voyage] in 1641 to be particularly high...the rewards of concealment, which were always great, were greater than usual this year. Some idea of the scale of fraud can be had... based on information from the mate, Francisco Granillo, who, being in charge of the stowage of the silver, should have some idea of the truth. 'The quantity [of silver] belonging to the King was large and an even greater quantity belonged to individuals who had not registered it, as there was no time and, as the masters preferred the risk to the registration, it was known that it [silver] was brought [onboard] without the necessary formalities.' Granillo's estimate of the total silver loaded on the *Concepción* was four million pesos, four times as great as that made by the official silver-master, weighing between 35 and 140 tons. It seems probable that the sum was nearer the upper than the lower bound.

Another interesting source regarding the value of treasure generally carried in Spanish plate vessels is that given by Dave Horner in his book *Shipwreck*, which relates to his own exciting experiences in working sunken wrecks. He writes:

After a thorough investigation of the registers of the *Carrera de las Indias*, Dr. Earl Hamilton calculated that between the years 1503 and 1660, a total of 447,820,931 pesos of registered treasure was reported being brought into Spain. This figure was based on a tally of 117,386,086 pesos for His Majesty, and 330,434,845 for private accounts. If this large sum was the officially registered total, one can only speculate as to the real value of silver, gold, emeralds, diamonds, pearls and all the many other goods entering outside of registry.

In connection with another legendary wreck, the *Nuestra Señora de las Maravillas*, which sank in 1656, Horner notes the following, which might equally apply to the *Concepción*:

> When one considers the gold and silver coin, the emeralds and other jewels, the highly crafted rosaries and crosses, and the many tons of hand-fashioned, worked silver which was recovered, but never reported, it is easy to see why the *Nuestra Señora de las Maravillas* is today, and always has been, one of the world's great lost treasure ships.

It is understandable why the evidence of sailors such as Granillo, who was in charge of stowing silver, relates to this commodity. Silver was the prime commodity transported to Spain on most vessels, and the importance of proper stowage for the voyage was paramount, as improper stowage could imperil the ship. This does not mean that other precious commodities did not constitute part of the cargo; they did, and were carried in large volumes, as indicated by the foregoing. However, silver was the most important, as it underpinned the economy of Spain. Granillo mentions none of this additional wealth in his statement, as his duties relate to the stowage of silver. But as far as the *Concepción* is concerned, apart from the silver in the form of minted coin, coin blanks and ingots of varying purity, there would have been a large number of other valuables in the form of plate, jewels, gemstones and Chinese trade goods, for the Spaniards had a virtual monopoly on trade with the Orient via their Pacific Fleet. Pearls, emeralds and lapis lazuli would have constituted an important and, possibly, an intrinsically more valuable part of the cargo.

We know that William Phips, following his discovery of the wreck of the *Concepción* off the coast of Hispaniola in 1687, recovered twenty-five tons of silver. Furthermore, we know that others recovered an additional five tons following Phips's departure from the wreck. The *Concepción* had broken amidships after foundering upon a reef, with the stern being carried over the reef to sink some five hundred feet distant from the bow. The recovery of silver — and only silver — is meaningful as this indicates that Phips, on his discovery of the wreck, only located the bow, for it was within the bow where the Spaniards stowed the less valuable cargo, unless it was needed elsewhere to supplement ballast.

Plate, jewellery, gemstones and other more valuable commodities were invariably confined to the stern, along with the private riches of the more privileged passengers stored in their cabins on the poop decks. It is the stern section that was the focus of the return expedition by Phips in 1687–88.

Regardless of how much silver was in the cargo of the *Concepción* — and according to Earle this would likely approximate to one hundred tons — it is certain that most of the bullion, if not all of that recovered by Phips during the return visit to the wreck, would have gone towards financing the invasion of England. This leaves the non-perishable goods constituting the balance of the cargo, not easily rendered into specie. It is this part of the cargo carried by the *Concepción* that we conclude as having been lost within the Money Pit: gemstones, jewels, plate and trade goods.

It is difficult, under the circumstances, to assess the value of the lost treasure, as it includes both official and contraband merchandise, and recovered artifacts in the form of jewels and plate commanding higher valuations. The twenty-five tons of silver (66,020 troy pounds) recovered by Phips after his discovery of the wreck in 1687, was valued at £205,500 (or £3 per troy pound). Based on the price of silver today

— about $30 per ounce — that would be worth approximately $30 million.

If we assume the *Concepción* carried one hundred tons of silver as its main cargo, with a mixed cargo of nonperishables of the same worth, i.e. gold bullion, plate, jewelled artifacts, gemstones, including emeralds, lapis lazuli and pearls, the total value of the cargo would be evaluated today at about $240 million. Allowing for all silver bullion to have been removed, i.e. twenty-five tons taken to England by Phips after the first visit to the wreck, and the remainder (seventy-five tons) taken to Holland by Mordaunt after the return to the wreck, the maximum value of treasure available for storage in the Money Pit would be approximately $120 million, i.e. half the value of the cargo. But this must be reduced further by an unknown amount to allow for all gold bullion removed during the second visit, which was also taken to Holland. Since we have no knowledge how much gold was carried by the *Concepción*, it is impossible to assess its worth. But assuming one-eighth of the total cargo did consist of gold bullion it would have possessed a value of about $30 million. Therefore, the value of the treasure consigned to the Money Pit may have been as high as $90 million in today's terms. However, we would suggest a figure of $60 million to allow for the uncertainties in this crude evaluation. As has been mentioned already, such estimates are fraught with uncertainty, but it is significant that the British Government expended a great deal of effort between 1752 and 1754 attempting to ensure that the lost treasure of William Phips remained buried for posterity. That act alone is indicative of its great worth.

To whom does the treasure belong? This is a hypothetical question at the present time, but could be of importance if it is ever recovered. The recovery of any large quantity of treasure is likely to spur claims by third parties, and the greater the treasure the deeper the litigious quagmire. It may be argued that, since the lost treasure of Oak Island was originally deposited by Phips on behalf of William, Prince of Orange, subsequently King William III, and since Queen Elizabeth is the latest monarch in an unbroken line following William's accession, the treasure belongs to the Crown, and through the Crown to the people of Nova Scotia.

If the people of Nova Scotia are to benefit from any successful future recovery effort, the government of the province will need to assert its ownership by clear and unequivocal legislation that will eliminate any subsequent contention of ownership.

Glossary

AMALGAM

A compound of mercury with another metal.

ANHYDRITE

A relatively soft, colourless to whitish-grey or lilac-coloured, evaporitic rock. Chemical formula $CaSO_4$. Found frequently associated with gypsum and salt in sedimentary rock formations, all of which are derived from evaporation of sea water.

BASALT

A very hard volcanic rock formed from solidified lava. Generally dark grey to black in colour, its surface weathers brown.

BECKER DRILL

A large drill that advances a casing of double wall construction using a pile-driving hammer. During driving, compressed air is continuously forced down the annular space and returned up the inside casing. The air stream picks up material (as large as three inches) as it enters through the advancing bit. The material is quickly lifted to the surface where it is collected for examination.

BLOW-OUT

A mining term indicating a catastrophic event when the external hydrostatic or rock pressure causes a failure of the rock environment in which mining is taking place. The mine workings become inundated with water and debris as a consequence. This type of event often leads to loss of life.

BULKHEAD

A construction, generally of timber, formed to protect an underground chamber from the inflow of dirt and water.

CARBON DATING

A method of dating organic material by determining the remnant amount of carbon-14 present. After the death of an organism, decay of the carbon-14 isotope ensues. By measuring the emission of radiation it is possible to determine the approximate period of time that has elapsed since the organism died.

CAULKING

The blocking of a seam or crack to make it watertight by driving in fibre, often pre-treated with tar or other water-resistant material.

CEMENT (Oak Island Context)

A form of mortar made from lime, water and sand. The lime (CaO) would be obtained by heating natural limestone to drive off excess carbon dioxide and then pulverising the clinker to form lime powder. The powder, when mixed with water to form a lime paste, could be mixed with sand to form an effective mortar.

CEMENT (Modern Usage)

Manufactured from limestone with varying proportions of slag to produce a powder, which when wetted will yield a hard, cementitious material. Portland cement is the term given to the commonest form in current usage.

COFFERDAM

A structure, usually constructed above ground, generally composed of timber, soil or rock, which isolates an area which is to be dewatered.

CORAL

A hard, limey substance built up in tropical seas by zoophytes, or marine polyps. Corals can assume many varieties and shapes, often of a fantastic nature.

CRIBBING

A closed form of timbering used in shaft sinking in soft, yielding ground.

DOLLAR

The Spanish dollar, or *real de a ocho*, is the famous 'piece-of-eight.'

DOLOMITE

A metamorphic variety of limestone, often containing a varying amount of magnesium. It is generally very hard and resistant.

EEL GRASS
A member of the *Zosteraceae* family, which is spread worldwide. It exists only in saltwater environments. It is of little economic importance, but was once used as packing and for cushion stuffing.

GLACIAL DRIFT
See glacial till.

GLACIAL ERRATICS
Boulders caught up by glacial movement and incorporated within the glacial till. Erratics may be transported long distances from their points of origin. The study of the composition and trails left by erratics is an important branch of glaciology and greatly aids in the interpretation of glacial movements.

GLACIAL TILL
A fairly uniform mixture of the various soils and remnant rock fragments caught up by glacial ice movement. The composition of the till is an important indicator to previous ice movements. Many tills reflect a composition similar to that of the local rock types. Till is often dense due to consolidation by the weight of ice and, because of its wide grain size distribution, is usually relatively impervious.

GLORY HOLE
A large hole, either at the surface or underground. When used to describe a surface feature the term is often derogative, thereby suggesting a large excavation made in an irresponsible and non-engineered fashion.

GRANITE
A hard rock of igneous origin, with a significant quartz content. The crystalline nature of the rock is clearly evident to the naked eye.

GYPSUM
A soft, colourless to white-grey rock. Chemical formula $CaSO_4.2H_2O$. Gypsum may be formed from anhydrite by hydration under low pressure, during which process it expands considerably, thereby creating much fracturing. Gypsum may be dehydrated under pressure and transformed back to the original anhydrite.

HEARTWOOD

The older central part of a tree.

HYDROSTATIC PRESSURE

The pressure resulting from the height of water above the point in question.

IGNEOUS ROCKS

Rocks that have originated from the cooling of hot, liquid rock. Where this cooling occurs at great depth it forms rocks exhibiting a well-developed crystalline texture, e.g. granite. Where cooling is rapid the texture is often amorphous, e.g. basalt.

INVERT

A tunnelling term for the base or floor of a tunnel.

LAPIS LAZULI

A rare silicate mineral of a rich azure-blue colour. The best occurrences are in Central Asia, where large masses are encountered. It is much esteemed for inlay work of an ornamental nature and jewelry. It is the 'sapphire of the ancients,' and should not be confused with common sapphire, which is a form of corundum and an oxide, and considerably harder than lapis.

LIME

Chemical symbol CaO. Obtained by heating natural limestone to drive off excess carbon dioxide.

LIME MORTAR

A mortar produced by wetting of lime to form a paste, then mixing with sand to produce a hard, rapid-setting material.

LIMESTONE

A widely distributed sedimentary rock having the chemical composition $CaCO_3$. The degree of hardness can vary considerably.

MANILLA GRASS

A corruption of manna grass. A member of the *Gramineae* family, genus

Glyceria. Sea meadow grass (*G.maritima*) is very common in Nova Scotia, where it is found in marshy saltwater habitats. Reed meadow grass (*G.aquatica*) prefers a freshwater environment.

METAMORPHIC ROCKS
Rocks of considerably different physical properties from their parents, after having been subjected to intense pressure and/or heat.

PESO
See dollar.

PIECE OF EIGHT
See dollar.

PORPHYRY
An igneous rock texture in which large crystals are set within a very fine-grained matrix.

PUDDLED CLAY
Clay that is deliberately wetted and reworked by mechanical means to obtain a plasticity suitable for forming plugs and seals.

QUICKSAND
A condition in which fully saturated, or waterlogged, sand 'runs' in an uncontrollable manner, or 'boils' because of the excessive hydrostatic pressure to which it is subjected. This pressure is always greater than the weight of the sand, thereby causing fluidity. It is a much misused and misapplied term, and applied to a number of situations that have little relation to true quicksand conditions.

SAPWOOD
The outer, younger part of a tree through which the sap moves to provide nutrients.

SEDIMENTARY ROCKS
Rock types laid down in the form of sediments as a consequence of erosion

of other rock types. Common sedimentary rock types are shale, mudstone, siltstone and sandstone. Limestone, gypsum, anhydrite and coal are also considered to be within this class.

SHALLOP

A large, heavy boat fitted with one or more masts.

SHEARING

The fracturing of rock by imposed stresses. These stresses may be tensile, compressive, slippage or bending or various combinations. Regardless of the nature of the imposed stress the rock will fracture if its strength is exceeded.

SINKHOLE

A hole that has been created by solution of water-soluble rock into which overlying soil has collapsed.

SLATE

A metamorphic rock produced from shale. It is often extremely hard and fissile, i.e. it has a pronounced tendency to part easily into thin, platelike fragments.

SOLLER

A false invert to a tunnel formed by sealed planks. Foul air and drainage water are extracted through the soller.

SOLUTION CHANNEL

A continuous pipelike feature within water-soluble rock that has been formed by percolating water. Solution channels often follow the path of fracturing within the rock, or other weaknesses that can be enlarged through solution.

SPILE

Wood or iron that has been driven into soft ground ahead of excavation to provide a measure of support while excavation takes place.

STRATUM

A layer of soil or rock that possesses common properties and characteristics.

TREENAIL/TRENAIL/TRENNEL

A long wooden pin or dowel, used for fastening planking and timbering on ships.

VOLCANIC ROCKS

Igneous rock types that have originated from the cooling of lavas ejected from volcanoes, e.g. basalt. The term also includes consolidated ashes and ejecta. Volcanic rocks are invariably extremely fine-grained as a consequence of the rapid cooling that the lava has experienced. There is no apparent crystallinity to the naked eye.

Bibliography

Books about Oak Island

[no author} *The Story of Oak Island*. Stoughton, Massachusetts: Record Publishing Co., 1895, 14 pages and two figures.
The first part of this booklet is a statement by Adams A. Tupper made in November 1893 describing the work at the Money Pit from 1795 to 1878 and the plans of the Oak Island Treasure Company. The second part gives additional historical information on the work of the Halifax Company in 1866–67 and the collapse of the Money Pit in 1861 as well as a description of the work done in 1894.

Crooker, William S., *The Oak Island Quest*. Hantsport, Nova Scotia: Lancelot Press, 1978, 194 pages.
The first one-third of this book includes a history of the findings at Oak Island up to the early 1970s. The middle part of the book presents a discussion of the findings with reference to issues such as the age of oak trees, the presence of ring-bolts for mooring ships, the stone triangle and the possibility of an offset treasure chamber. The last part of the book reviews many of the popular theories to explain the Oak Island workings and advances other theories related to ancient or extraterrestrial civilisations. The author's preferred theory is that the workings were created by a past civilisation of advanced capability.

Crooker, William S., *Oak Island Gold*. Halifax, Nova Scotia: Nimbus Publishing, 1993, 221 pages.
In his second book on Oak Island, Crooker updates exploration efforts at the Money Pit and again reviews most of the popular theories. He acknowledges that the preferred theory in his first book is rather far-fetched. The stone cross (huge boulders in the pattern of a cross) identified by Fred Nolan's surveys in the north-central part of Oak Island is introduced together with speculations on a Knights Templar connection.

Crooker presents a preferred theory suggesting, based on circumstantial evidence, that senior members of the British military conspired to bury on Oak Island part of the treasure obtained from the sack of Havana in 1762.

Evans, Millie, and Mullen, Eric, *Oak Island Nova Scotia: The World's Greatest Treasure Hunt.* Tantallon, Nova Scotia: Four East Publications, 1984, 58 pages.
This book, as acknowledged by the authors, is a simplified and short account of the Oak Island story.

Evans, Millie, *Nova Scotia's Oak Island: The Unsolved Mystery.* Tantallon, Nova Scotia: Four East Publications, 1993, 44 pages.
Evans provides a straightforward and brief review of the search for treasure on Oak Island.

Fanthorpe, Lionel and Patricia, *The Oak Island Mystery: The Secret of the World's Greatest Treasure Hunt.* Toronto: Hounslow Press, 1995, 221 pages.
The Fanthorpes give an account of Oak Island explorations and the most popular theories. In addition theories are presented related to the Celts and Vikings, Mediterranean traders from the fourth century BC, the Knights Templar, Prince Henry Sinclair, Sir Francis Drake and others. It is postulated that Oak Island is the repository for a number of treasures and invaluable sacred objects.

Finnan, Mark, *Oak Island Secrets.* Halifax, Nova Scotia: Formac Publishing, Revised Edition, 1997, 178 pages. First published in 1995.
Finnan provides a review of the history of the explorations and findings on Oak Island with particular emphasis on the stone cross and other artifacts found by Fred Nolan. Finnan briefly reviews the theories of other research-ers and concludes, based on the stone cross and other artifacts, that there is a Masonic connection to the mystery. He further concludes that Oak Island is the repository for a sacred treasure, which was deposited in the late sixteenth century under the overall direction of Sir Francis Bacon. The

revised edition contains a two-page epilogue but is otherwise the same as the first edition.

Furneaux, Rupert, *Money Pit: The Mystery of Oak Island.* London and Toronto: Fontana, 1976, 158 pages. First published in 1972 as *The Money Pit Mystery: The Costliest Treasure Hunt Ever.*
Rupert Furneaux spent seven years investigating the Oak Island mystery and the first two-thirds of the book provides a detailed account of exploration activities up to the early 1970s. He makes a connection between the Roper survey and the variation in magnetic declination with time to suggest that the works on Oak Island were carried out about the year 1780. Furneaux concludes that senior members of the British military in North America clandestinely transferred large sums of money from New York for concealment on Oak Island. He suggests that the treasure is buried in an offset chamber. He argues that the presence of a British military and naval force on Oak Island may not have seemed strange to the residents of the area, thus it was not recorded as an exceptional event. The first publication of the book in hardcover is identical to the second publication in paperback.

Harris, Reginald V., *The Oak Island Mystery.* Toronto: The Ryerson Press, June 1958, 211 pages.
This is the first comprehensive and complete published account of the operations on Oak Island available to the general public. Harris extends the story up to the work of George Green in 1955. Harris also provides a brief review of the many theories in circulation at that time but does not offer a preference. The book is based on many original documents that are no longer available and thus represents a valuable record of the work on Oak Island.

Harris, Reginald V., *The Oak Island Mystery.* Toronto: McGraw-Hill Ryerson, second edition, 1967, 209 pages.
This book is a completely revised and updated version of the first edition and extends up to the work of Dunfield in 1967. Again, this book is a valuable record of the early explorations at Oak Island.

Johnson, Laverne, *Revealed: The Secret of Oak Island.* Vancouver: Benwell Atkins, 1991, 32 pages.
Johnson provides a brief history of the search for treasure and offers his opinion on where the treasure is buried. He suggests that the flood system protects the entrance of a deeper offset tunnel running up into the higher ground 300 feet to the north with the treasure being located 20 feet below undisturbed ground. The plan location of the treasure is based on triangulation from the stone triangle and drilled rocks, but Johnson's drilling program in 1965 found only natural soil in this area. He indicates that the treasure originates from Central America and was brought to Oak Island by ship some time before 1749.

Lamb, Lee, *Oak Island Obsession: The Restall Story.* Toronto: The Dundurn Group, 2006, 242 pages.
Lee lamb gives a personal account of the search for treasure by the Restall family from 1960 to 1966. The book includes interesting correspondence, sketches, and photos not previously published. Also a retrospective is given of the tragic accident that claimed the lives of two members of the family.

Lamb, Lee, *Oak Island Family: The Restall Hunt for Buried Treasure.* Toronto: Dundurn, 2012, 132 pages.
Lee Lamb writes a simplified version of the Restall family treasure hunt for the benefit of a younger audience.

Leary, Thomas P., *The Oak Island Enigma.* Omaha, Nebraska: Leary publications, 1953, 36 pages.
Part I of the book provides a summary of the work on Oak Island and Part II provides brief comments on the various parties who may have dug the Money Pit. Part II also presents Leary's theory that the treasure consists of the lost manuscripts of Sir Francis Bacon.

Marcil, Claude, and Paul, Françoise, *Oak Island: L'Île au Trésor.* Chicoutimi, Québéc and Ottawa, Ontario: Les Éditions JCL Inc., 1989, 125 pages (in French).

Marcil and Paul provide a review of the search for treasure and present the popular theories. In addition they speculate that part of the storm damaged French fleet (dispatched to retake Louisbourg in 1746) buried treasure on Oak Island.

O'Connor, D'Arcy, *The Money Pit: The Story of Oak Island and the World's Greatest Treasure Hunt.* New York: Coward, McCann and Geohagen, 1978, 256 pages.
(see below)

O'Connor, D'Arcy, *The Big Dig: The $10 Million Search for Oak Island's Legendary Treasure.* New York: Ballantine Books, 1988, 258 pages.
O'Connor provides a revision and update of his previous work giving the most complete and detailed history of the explorations on Oak Island available in one document. Also he provides interesting and credible commentary on many of the popular Oak Island theories and historical issues. His preferred theory is that sometime around 1600 a storm-damaged Spanish galleon, separated from the rest of the fleet, buried treasure at Oak Island. The ship was sufficiently repaired to set out for Spain, with the intention of coming back for the treasure, but sank en route and was lost without trace.

O'Connor, D'Arcy, *The Secret Treasure of Oak Island: The Amazing True Story of a Centuries-Old Treasure.* Guilford, Connecticut: The Lyons Press, 2004, 279 pages.
O'Connor provides another excellent revision and update of his previous work. Many additions are made to previous material and the story is brought up to date. O'Connor stays with his preferred theory of the storm-damaged Spanish galleon.

Sora, Steven, *The Lost Treasure of the Knights Templar: Solving the Oak Island Mystery.* Rochester, Vermont: Destiny Books, 1999, 293 pages.
Steven Sora provides a brief review of findings by different searchers and presents the popular theories put forward to explain the Oak Island mystery. He then sets the stage for his theory with a detailed account of the

1398 voyage of Prince Henry Sinclair from the Orkney Islands in Northern Scotland to present day Nova Scotia, followed by a history of the Sinclair Clan. Sora claims that much of the treasure of the Knights Templar was transferred to the custody of the Sinclair Clan in Scotland after the order was disbanded in 1307. He describes a scenario where William Sinclair, the grandson of Prince Henry, prepared a vault on Oak Island between 1436 and 1441, with transfer of the treasure occurring somewhere between 1441 and 1482.

Technical Reports on Oak Island

Blankenship, Dan, *Periodic Reports on Oak Island Operations 1966 to 1994*, compiled by Les MacPhie. Private publication, July 2012.

Canada Cement Lafarge Ltd., Montreal, Quebec, *Oak Island Samples: Project 20722*. Report by W.S. Weaver and Dr. H. Chen to David Tobias, March 14, 1977.

Cox Underground Research Limited, *The Oak Island Exploration: A Project of Triton Alliance Ltd.: Engineering and Operational Plans Including Cost Estimates.* Westmount, Quebec, 1987.

Fader, G.B.J., and Courtney, R.C., *An Interpretation of Multibeam Bathymetry off Eastern Oak Island, Mahone Bay, Nova Scotia.* Geological Survey of Canada (Atlantic), Bedford Institute of Oceanography. Issued April 1998.

Golder Associates, *Subsurface Investigation, The Oak Island Exploration, Oak Island, Nova Scotia.* Draft Report No. 69126 to Triton Alliance Ltd., Montreal, Quebec, April 28, 1971.

Parkin, Bill, *Figures of Sonar Profiles on Oak Island.* Report to David Tobias on Bedrock Cavity at 10X, October 6, 1989.

Ritchie, J.C., Professor of Biology, *Report on Palynological Analyses of Four (4) Samples from The Oak Island Exploration.* Dalhousie University Project 69126, May 25, 1970.

Smithsonian Institution, Washington, D.C., *Examination of Artifacts.* Report to David Tobias by M.L. Peterson, Chairman, Department of Armed Forces History, December 22, 1967.

The Steel Company of Canada, Hamilton, Ontario, *Examination and Analysis of Metal Artifacts from Oak Island.* Reports by Allan B. Dove, Senior Development Metallurgist, dated March 11, 1970; August 18, 1970; September 25, 1970; November 19, 1970; December 14, 1970; March 30, 1971; and April 22, 1971.

Warnock Hersey International Limited, *Soils Investigation, Oak Island, Nova Scotia.* Report No. 530-110 to Carr & Donald & Associates, Toronto Ontario, July 31, 1969 and November 5, 1969.

Woods Hole Oceanographic Institution, Woods Hole, Maine, *Oak Island Hydrogeology, Hydrography and Nearshore Morphology, July – August 1995 Field Observations.* Draft Report by David G. Aubrey, Wayne D. Spencer, Ben Guiterez, William Robertson and David Gallo, April 8, 1996.

Articles about Oak Island

Bowdoin, H.L., "Solving the Mystery of Oak Island: The Hundred-Year Search for the $10,000,000 Supposed to Have Been Buried by Pirates," *Collier's Magazine,* August 18, 1911.

Harris, Graham, "Recovering the Oak Island Treasure," *Imperial College Engineer,* Issue 31, Spring 2002, — see also www.cgca.org.uk/magazine/spring2002.

Harris, Graham, "The Oak Island Treasure: The Military Cover-Up 1752–54." An address to the Oak Island Tourism Society. Private publication, 2007.

Harris, Graham, "The Oak Island Cofferdam." *Imperial Engineer*, Issue Eleven, Autumn 2009. See also: http://www.cgca.org.uk/magazine/autumn2009.

Harris, Graham, "The Treasure and Treason of William Phips." *No Quarter Given*, September 2004 to January 2005.

Liverpool Transcript, "The Oak Island Diggings." October 16, 1862.

Morell, Parker, "The Money Pit." *The Saturday Evening Post*, October 14, 1939.

Preston, Douglas, "The Mysterious Money Pit." *Smithsonian*, Vol.19, No.3, June, 1988.

Rosenbaum, Ron, "The Mystery of Oak Island." *Esquire*, February, 1973.

Sullivan, Randall, "The Curse of Oak Island." *Rolling Stone Magazine*, January 22, 2004.

Taylor, Michael, "Yep, They're Still Digging." *Forbes FYI*, September 25, 1995.

The Colonist, "History of the Oak Island Enterprise: Chapters I and II." January 2 and 7, 1864.

The Hamilton Spectator, "The Riddle of Oak Island: Gold Bars Within My Grasp Says Bob Restall." Friday, January 29, 1965.

The Novascotian, "The Oak Island Folly." September 30, 1861.

Wroclawski, Paul, "Essential History of Oak Island to 1795 (Draft)."
www.oakislandtheories.com, February 2013, 77 pages.

Other References

Agricola, Georgius, *De Re Metallica*. Translated from the First Latin
edition of 1556 by Herbert Clark Hoover and Lou Henry Hoover. New
York: Dover Publications, 1950.

Baker, Emerson W., and Reid, John G., *The New England Knight*.
Toronto: University of Toronto Press, 1998.

Barnes, Neal E., and Piper, David J.W., "Late Quaternary Geological
History of Mahone Bay, Nova Scotia." *Canadian Journal of Earth
Sciences*, Vol. 15, 1978, pages 586-593.

Barrie, Alexander, *War Underground: The Tunnellers of the Great War*.
London: Tom Donovan Publishing, 1988 (First published in 1962).

Barton, Peter, Doyle, Peter, and Vandewalle, Johan, *Beneath Flanders
Fields: The Tunnellers' War 1914-18*. Staplehurst, Kent: Spellmount
Limited, 2004.

Bevan, Bryan, *King William III*. London: The Rubicon Press, 1997.

Bowden, Tracy, "Treasure From the Silver Bank." *National Geographic*,
July, 1996.

Connolly, Thomas W.J., *The History of the Corps of Royal Sappers and
Miners*. London: Longman, Brown, Green & Longmans, 1855.

DesBrisay, Mather Byles, *History of the County of Lunenburg*. Belleville,
Ontario: Mika Studio, facsimile edition, 1972. Originally published in
1895 by William Briggs, Toronto.

Duffy, Christopher, *Fire and Stone: The Science of Fortress Warfare 1660–1860*. Edison, New Jersey: Castle Books, 2006, 207 pages (First published in 1975).

Duncan, Roger, *Coastal Maine: A Maritime History*. New York: W.W. Norton & Company, 1992.

Dunn, Brenda, *A History of Port Royal/Annapolis Royal: 1605-1800*. Halifax, Nova Scotia: Nimbus Publishing Limited and The Historical Association of Annapolis Royal, 2004, 286 pages.

Dyer, Florence E., *The Life of Admiral Sir John Narbrough: that Great Commander and Able Seaman*. London: Philip Allan, 1931.

Earle, Peter, *The Treasure of the Concepción: The Wreck of the Almiranta*. New York: The Viking Press, 1980. First published in England under the title *The Wreck of the Almiranta*.

Eckel, Edwin C., *Cements, Limes, and Plasters: Their Materials, Manufacture and Properties*. New York: John Wiley & Sons, 1907.

Giles, P.S., *The Windsor Group of the Mahone Bay Area, Nova Scotia*. Nova Scotia Department of Mines and Energy, Paper 81-3, 1981.

Greenwood, John and Price, Robert, "Locating Underground Features by Dowsing." *Ground Engineering, the Magazine of the British Geotechnical Association*, Volume 34, Number 1, January 2001.

Grissim, John, *The Lost Treasure of the Concepción: The Story of One of the World's Greatest Treasure Finds and Baurt Webber—The Man Who Never Gave Up*. New York: William Morrow and Company, 1980.

Harris, Graham, *Treasure and Intrigue: The Legacy of Captain Kidd.* Toronto: Dundurn Press, 2002.

Harris, Graham, *The Golden Reef of Sir William Phips*, Charleston: Booksurge Publishing, 2005.

Horner, Dave, *Shipwreck: A saga of Sea Tragedy and Sunken Treasure.* Dobbs Ferry, New York: Sheridan House, 1999, 295 pages.

Hornsby, Stephen J., *Surveyors of Empire: Samuel Holland, J. F. W. Des Barres, and the Making of the Atlantic Neptune.* Montreal & Kingston, London, Ithaca: McGill-Queen's University Press, 2011, 269 pages.

Hunt, Robert, *British Mining: A Treatise on the History, Discovery, Practical Development and Future Prospects of Metalliferous Mines in the United Kingdom.* London: Crosby Lockwood and Co., 1884.

James, A.N., *Soluble Materials in Civil Engineering.* London: Ellis Horwood, 1992.

James, A.N., and Lupton, A.R.R., "Gypsum and Anhydrite in Foundations of Hydraulic Structures." *Geotechnique*, The Institution of Civil Engineers, London, Vol. 28, Sept. 1978, pages 249-272.

Karraker, Cyrus H., *The Hispaniola Treasure.* Philadelphia: University of Pennsylvania Press, 1934.

Leslie, Sir Stephen, and Lee, Sir Sidney (Ed.), *Dictionary of National Biography: From the Earliest Times to 1990.* (22 volumes). London: Oxford University Press, 1885-1901.

Lounsberry, Alice, *Sir William Phips: Treasure Fisherman and Governor of Massachusetts Bay.* New York: Charles Scribners & Sons, 1941.

Macaulay, Thomas B., *The History of England (5 volumes)*. Boston: Aldine Publishing, first published 1848.

McCreath, Peter L., and Leefe, John G., *A History of Early Nova Scotia*. Tantallon, Nova Scotia: Four East Publications, 1982.

Mercer, Henry C., *Ancient Carpenters' Tools: Together with Lumberman's, Joiners' and Cabinet Makers' Tools in Use in the Eighteenth Century*. Pennsylvania: Horizon Press, published for the Bucks County Historical Society, Fifth Edition 1975, first published 1929.

Moray, Sir Robert, *An Account how Adits & Mines are Wrought at Liège without Air Shafts*. Philosophical Transactions of the Royal Society of London, Volume 1, No. 5, July 3, 1665.

Morgan, William, *Mining Tools*. London: Lockwood and Co, 1891, pp. 72–93.

Newspaper reports on ship arrivals/departures information for Falmouth:

The General Advertiser (July 2, 1752) "Falmouth, June 28—Carrick Roads—a large ship unknown with Palatines."

The General Advertiser (July 4, 1752) "The ship is identified as the Gale, Casson, with Palatines for Nova Scotia."

The General Advertiser (July 7, 1752) "July 2—sailed the Gale, Casson, for Nova Scotia."

The London Daily Advertiser (July 2, 1752) "By letter dated June 27th we have advice that a large ship with Palatine passengers aboard for America, was put into Carrick Road."

The London Daily Advertiser (July 7, 1752) reports "…the sailing of the Gale, Casson, for Nova Scotia on July 2nd."

Ogg, David, *William III*. New York: Collier Books, 1967.

Porter, Whitworth, *History of the Corps of Royal Engineers (Vol. I)*. London: Longmans & Green, 1889.

Ross, Sally, and Deveau, Alphonse, *The Acadians of Nova Scotia: Past and Present*. Halifax, Nova Scotia: Nimbus Publishing, 1992.

Stea, R.R., and Brown, Y., "Variation in Drumlin Orientation, Form and Stratigraphy Relating to Successive Ice Flows in Southern and Central Nova Scotia." *Sedimentary Geology*, 62, 1989, pages 223-240.

Stea, Rudolph R., Fader, Gordon B.J., Scott, David B., and Wu, Patrick, "Glacial and Relative Sea-level Change in Maritime Canada." In Weddle, T.K. and Retelle, M.J., eds., *Deglacial History and Relative Sea-Level Changes: Northern New England and Adjacent Canada*. Boulder, Colorado, Geological Society of America Special Paper 351, 2001, pages 35–49.

Wallace-Murphy, Tim, and Hopkins, Marilyn, *Templars in America: From the Crusades to the New World*. Boston, MA/York Beach, ME: Weiser Books, 2004.

Ward, Estelle F., *Christopher Monck Duke of Albemarle*, London: John Murray, 1915.

White, Neil J., Church, John A., and Gregory, Jonathan M., 2005. *Coastal and Global Averaged Sea Level Rise for 1950 to 2000*. American Geophysical Union, Geophysical Research Letters, Vol. 32, 2005.

Wilkins, Harold T., *Captain Kidd and His Skeleton Island*. New York: Liverwright Publishing Corp., 1937.

Appendix

Note: Reference should be made to Figures 12, 14, 15, 19, 22 and 24
for shaft and excavation locations.

Item	Group	Year	Depth (feet)	Location	Remarks
Shaft 1	McGinnis, Smith and Vaughan	1795	25 (or 30)	Money Pit	Digging stopped due to lack of assistance
Shaft 1	Onslow Syndicate	1804	93	Money Pit	Flooded and bailing not successful
Shaft 2	Onslow Syndicate	1805	110	14 feet southeast (or east) of Money Pit	Lateral tunnel toward Money Pit flooded (See Fig. 9 and 10)
Shaft 1	Truro Syndicate	1849	86	Money Pit	Flooded and bailing not successful
Drilling	Truro Syndicate	1849	106 to 112	Money Pit	Five auger holes drilled, assumed timber platforms and metal pieces in oak chests encountered from 98 to 105 feet (See Fig. 11)
Shaft 3	Truro Syndicate	1850	109	Tupper Pit located 10 feet northwest (or west) of Money Pit	Lateral tunnel toward Money Pit flooded

Item	Group	Year	Depth (feet)	Location	Remarks
Excavation	Truro Syndicate	1850	—	Smith's Cove	Cofferdam constructed to expose filter bed and feeder drains within tidal range (See Fig. 12 and 13)
Shaft 4	Truro Syndicate	1850	75	100 feet from beach at Smith's Cove	Attempt to intersect Flood Tunnel after finding filter drain at Smith's Cove, no water encountered
Shaft 5	Truro Syndicate	1850	80 (or 35)	12 feet south of Shaft No. 4	Flooded on removal of large boulder at 80 feet (or 35 feet)
Shaft 5A	Truro Syndicate	1850	112	Slightly west of Money Pit	Lateral tunnel toward Money Pit flooded
Shaft 1	Oak Island Association	1861	88	Money Pit	Cleaned out and cribbed to 88 feet
Shaft 5B	Oak Island Association	1861	120	25 feet east of Money Pit	Attempt to intersect Flood Tunnel, no water encountered
Shaft 6	Oak Island Association	1861	118	18 feet west (or south) of Money Pit	Lateral tunnel toward Money Pit, collapse of cribbing and platforms in Money Pit, dewatering with steam driven pump not successful
Shaft 7	Oak Island Association	1862	107	Directly west of Money Pit	Used as a dewatering shaft for the steam driven pump

Item	Group	Year	Depth (feet)	Location	Remarks
Shaft 1	Oak Island Association	1862	103	Money Pit	Cleaned out and cribbed to 103 feet, found tools left by Onslow and Truro Syndicates
Shaft 8	Oak Island Association	1862	—	Near Shaft No. 6	Location and results not clear
Shaft 9	Oak Island Association	1863/64	120	100 feet east of Money Pit and 20 feet south of Flood Tunnel	Tunnels extended from bottom of shaft to locate Flood Tunnel but not successful
Excavation	Halifax Company	1866	—	Smith's Cove	Cofferdam constructed to excavate filter bed and feeder drains, cofferdam destroyed by sea action shortly after excavation started
Shaft 1	Halifax Company	1866	108	Money Pit	Cleaned out Money Pit
Drilling	Halifax Company	1866	up to 163	Money Pit	Drilled 3 holes from platform at a depth of 90 feet in Money Pit
Shaft 10	Halifax Company	1867	110	175 feet south of Flood Tunnel and 200 feet southeast of Money Pit	Extensive lateral tunnelling, found entrance of Flood Tunnel on east wall of Money Pit at a depth of 110 feet
Shaft 11	Sophia Sellers	1878	10	Cave-In Shaft 350 feet east of Money Pit	Ground subsided and team of oxen dropped into a hole 8 feet diameter by 10 feet deep

Item	Group	Year	Depth (feet)	Location	Remarks
Shaft 11	Oak Island Treasure Company	1894	55	Cave-In Shaft 350 feet east of Money Pit	Sea water entered at a depth of 55 feet to tide level and bailing could not lower water in shaft
Shaft 12	Oak Island Treasure Company	1894	55	30 feet east of Money Pit and 8 feet north of Flood Tunnel	Water entered at 43 feet and shaft abandoned after digging to 55 feet and tunnelling to south
Shaft 3	Oak Island Treasure Company	1895/ 97	110	10 feet northwest of Money Pit	Thought excavation was in Money Pit but realized in April, 1897 that excavation was in Shaft No. 3 (Tupper Pit)
Shaft 1	Oak Island Treasure Company	1897	111 (114 locally)	Money Pit	Found Flood Tunnel at 110 to 114 feet on east side of Money Pit
Drilling	Oak Island Treasure Company	1897	80 to 95	Near shore at Smith's Cove	5 holes drilled near shore at Smith's Cove to investigate Flood Tunnel (See Fig. 15 and 16)
Drilling	Oak Island Treasure Company	1897	132 to 188	Money Pit	5 holes drilled at Money Pit, assumed cement vault containing metal bars and coin encountered from 153 to 160 feet (See Fig. 17 and 18)
Shaft 13	Oak Island Treasure Company	1897	82	25 feet north of Cave-In Shaft	Lateral tunnel toward Cave-In Shaft flooded, eventually encountered an old Halifax tunnel

Item	Group	Year	Depth (feet)	Location	Remarks
Shaft 14	Oak Island Treasure Company	1897	95	45 feet south of Money Pit	Shaft abandoned at a depth of 95 feet due to water inflow from old tunnel at a depth of 70 feet
Shaft 15	Oak Island Treasure Company	1898	160	35 feet southwest of Shaft No. 14 and 80 feet from Money Pit	Water entered from a sand seam at 160 feet and shaft abandoned after pumping could not dewater shaft
Shaft 16	Oak Island Treasure Company	1898	134	100 feet north of Money Pit	Shaft abandoned due to quicksand and/or flooding
Shaft 17	Oak Island Treasure Company	1898	95	60 feet east of Money Pit	Shaft abandoned due to quicksand and/or flooding
Shaft 18	Oak Island Treasure Company	1898	160	15 feet southwest of Shaft No. 17	Shaft abandoned due to quicksand and/or flooding
Dye Test	Oak Island Treasure Company	1898	111	Money Pit	Dye test showed connection between Money Pit and South Shore Cove, second Flood Tunnel assumed
Shaft 19	Oak Island Treasure Company	1899	144	100 feet west of Money Pit	Shaft abandoned due to quicksand and/or flooding
Shaft 20	Oak Island Treasure Company	1900	113	Overlapping west side of Money Pit	Abandoned due to high water inflow at 113 feet

Item	Group	Year	Depth (feet)	Location	Remarks
Drilling	Oak Island Treasure Company	1900	126	In Money Pit	Drilled 8 auger holes
Shaft 1	Old Gold Salvage and Wrecking Company	1909	113	Money Pit	Cleaned out flooded Money Pit to 113 feet with clam bucket
Drilling	Old Gold Salvage and Wrecking Company	1909	155 to 171	In and around Money Pit	28 holes drilled from ground surface
Shaft 21	William Chappell and Frederick Blair	1931	155	Chappell Shaft on southwest side of Money Pit	Artifacts of original excavators found (See Fig. 20)
Drilling	William Chappell and Frederick Blair	1931	167	Chappell Shaft	Drilled holes to 12 feet below bottom of shaft and drilled some lateral holes at a depth of 130 feet
Drilling	Canadian Oak Island Treasure Company	1934	up to 176	Around Money Pit	Drilled 14 holes up to 176 feet deep, fragments of china found below 123 feet
Shaft 21	Gilbert Hedden	1936	160	Chappell Shaft	Chappell Shaft reinstated to previous depth of 155 feet and deepened to 160 feet
Shaft 22	Gilbert Hedden	1937	125	Hedden Shaft on northeast side of Money Pit	Shaft extended to 125 feet (See Fig. 20)

Item	Group	Year	Depth (feet)	Location	Remarks
Drilling	Gilbert Hedden	1937	167	Hedden Shaft	Drilling carried out for 42 feet below bottom of shaft
Drilling	Edwin Hamilton	1938	—	Hedden Shaft	Drilled 58 lateral holes at various depths in the Hedden Shaft
Shaft 21	Edwin Hamilton	1939	160	Chappell Shaft	Chappell Shaft retimbered to 160 feet
Shaft 22	Edwin Hamilton	1940	170	Hedden Shaft	6x6 foot segment on west side of Hedden Shaft deepened from 125 to 155 feet
Shaft 21	Edwin Hamilton	1941	167	Chappell Shaft	Chappell Shaft deepened from 160 to 167 feet where bedrock was found
Drilling	Edwin Hamilton	1941	below 200	Chappell Shaft	Drilled through bedrock from 167 feet to below 200 feet and chips of oak were brought up from the bedrock
Dye Test	Edwin Hamilton	1941	167	Chappell Shaft	Dye test showed connection to deep water in South Shore Cove
Drilling	George Greene	1955	up to 190	North of Chappell Shaft	Drilled four holes at distances of 2, 6, 10 and 14 feet north of Chappell Shaft

Item	Group	Year	Depth (feet)	Location	Remarks
Drilling	William and Victor Harman	1958	up to 212	At and around Money Pit	Recovered oak, spruce and coconut fibre from 150 feet and deeper
Excavation	Robert Restall	1960/ 65	—	Chappell and Hedden Shafts and Filter Bed at Smith's Cove	Explored Chappell and Hedden Shafts, dug 65 shallow pits in Filter Bed and excavated two shafts at Smith's Cove shoreline to about a depth of 25 feet
Excavation	Robert Dunfield	1965	20	South Shore	Excavated trench 200 feet long parallel to beach
Excavation	Robert Dunfield	1965	54	South Shore, 25 feet south of stone triangle	Excavated open pit at location of original 8 foot diameter backfilled shaft
Excavation	Robert Dunfield	1965/ 66	135	Money Pit	Excavated open pit 80 to 100 feet across at top and 135 feet deep at Money Pit, backfilled to allow access for drilling
Drilling	Robert Dunfield	1966	190	Money Pit	Drilled 6-inch diameter holes
Excavation	Robert Dunfield	1966	108	Cave-In Shaft	Excavated open pit to a depth of 108 feet at Cave-In Shaft

Item	Group	Year	Depth (feet)	Location	Remarks
Shaft	David Tobias and Dan Blankenship	1966	90	South Shore at original 8 foot diameter shaft	Found rounded granite boulders and stagnant water at 90 feet
Drilling	David Tobias and Dan Blankenship	1967	up to 250	In and around Money Pit	Deep holes by Becker Drills Limited found wood and cavities in bedrock and other artifacts
Drilling	Triton Alliance	1969	250	Around Money Pit	Deep holes by Warnock Hersey
Drilling	Triton Alliance	1970	250	Around Money Pit	Deep holes by Golder Associates
Excavation	Triton Alliance	1970	—	Smith's Cove	Cofferdam at Smith's Cove and timber structure encountered within tidal zone
Drilling	Triton Alliance	1970	235	Borehole 10X	Drilled in 6-inch diameter by rotary drilling then casing installed, encountered metal fragments
Shaft 10X	Triton Alliance	1970/71	235	Borehole 10X	Installed 27-inch diameter casing to bedrock at 181 feet and hole uncased to 230 feet, encountered metal and cement

Item	Group	Year	Depth (feet)	Location	Remarks
Inspection	Triton Alliance	1971/72	235	Borehole 10X	Inspection of cavity below 230 feet by underwater TV camera and diver
Drilling	Triton Alliance	1973	—	General area	Encountered wire at a depth of 110 feet in hole located 660 feet north of Money Pit
Triton Shaft	Triton Alliance	1973/74	100	Triton shaft, 660 feet north of Money Pit	Shaft abandoned due to water inflow along shaft
Shaft 10X	Triton Alliance	1978/80	126	Borehole 10X	Installed 8-foot diameter casing to 90 feet and concrete lining from 90 to 126 feet
Drilling	Triton Alliance	1983	590	Borehole 401, 200 feet north of Money Pit	Anhydrite bedrock from 181 feet, slate bedrock at 360 feet
Shaft 10X	Triton Alliance	1987/90	181	Borehole 10X	Deepened concrete lining from 126 to bedrock surface at 181 feet

Item	Group	Year	Depth (feet)	Location	Remarks
Drilling	Noon Star (by contract with Triton Alliance)	1999 and 2001	30 to 50	Approximately 40 Boreholes north of Money Pit	Search for offset chamber, found natural undisturbed ground
Test Pits by Backhoe	Petter Amundsen (by contract with Triton Alliance)	2003	3 to 6	South of Boulder Cross	Approximately four shallow test pits found different shaped boulders in the glacial till

Index